TONY HAND

A LIFE IN BRITISH ICE HOCKEY

TONY HAND

A LIFE IN BRITISH ICE HOCKEY

TONY HAND MBE WITH MIKE APPLETON

Dedicated to my family.
Without you I wouldn't be where I am today.

First published 2006

Stadia is an imprint of
Tempus Publishing Limited
The Mill, Brimscombe Port,
Stroud, Gloucestershire, GL5 2QG
www.tempus-publishing.com

© Tony Hand MBE and Mike Appleton, 2006

British Library Cataloguing in Publication Data.
A catalogue record for this book is available from the British Library.

ISBN 0 7524 3797 6

Typesetting and origination by Tempus Publishing Limited
Printed in Great Britain

CONTENTS

ACKNOWLEDGEMENTS

When you have been within a sport or any organisation for that matter for nigh on twenty-five years, it is very difficult to thank everyone who has put me in the position to write this book. But here goes; sorry for any omissions!

I would like to thank my family: mum and dad Lorraine and David, wife Melissa and my two kids Sarah and Paul, for all the love and support they have given me over the years.

I would also like to thank the coaches, players and officials who have been part of my career for so long, and the fans and sponsors of all the clubs I have played for.

For their help in putting this book together both myself and Mike would like to thank (in no particular order) Ian Mizen, Stewart Roberts of the *Ice Hockey Annual*, Ronnie Nichol, Norrie Tait, Glen Sather, Mark Tredgold, Paul Thompson, Rick Brebant, Ivan Matulik, Moray Hanson, Craig Mudie, Tony Boot, Dave Simms, Les Lovell, Bob Westerdale, Alex Dampier, Ed Courtenay and Nigel McFarlane.

FOREWORD BY PAUL THOMPSON

There will not be another British player that can dominate a mainly North American and Canadian hockey league the way Tony Hand MBE has for so many years. There, I've said it. Tony may not like me buttering him up, but this is my foreword and if he won't say these things, I will!

Tony remains possibly the most humble man I have ever met in sport and is a true friend. Twenty years ago everybody knew who Tony was and looked up to him – me included. He gave everyone hope and opened the door for British ice hockey.

I first played against him when I was a scrappy third liner at Solihull, and looking back, I was probably minus 10 in the first period. But Tony has always created his own hype. Players loved to compete against him and still do, even if they didn't and don't have much luck. Even now, when I speak to young kids during our hockey schools he still is the player they all want to be.

Throughout the past twenty-five years, the standards on the ice and the calibre of the leagues may have evolved, but a true athlete will rise to every level in front of them. It's fair to say that Tony hasn't just risen – he has led every level. Every year clubs, professionals and scouts have talked about the next big thing in British hockey, and while some players have shown promise, most have dipped away as the majority of clubs have looked to imported talent. But Tony's desire, passion and drive for the game has taken him to the top.

He has an unbelievable talent and vision for the game and he sees more than some players will ever see. But with all that he has never shirked the responsibility of being a top player.

Being at the top doesn't just come down to natural ability. You need drive and dedication. When we were away in Canada at a coaching convention with Simmsy (David Simms from Sheffield), breakfast was at 8 a.m. and Tony was out running the roads at 6 a.m. to find a gym. That shows the dedication he shows in striving to be the best.

Tony and I are very similar. We are very driven and I think if Tony played basketball, tennis or golf he would have the same attitude – he is a natural winner. But he will be the last player to talk about what he has done. It's not arrogance, or ignorance, but down to ambition.

And when you look back he has clocked up an incredible amount of ice time. At every team he has been a 'go to' player and with that comes the attentions of the opposition. He has had his fair share of whacks, elbows, slashes and cheap shots, week in, week out for years and you'll never see him crying off with flu, a twisted sock or sore ankle. Of course he will have these, but he loves being on the ice. No team can say that he has cheated them.

And to make the transition to player/coach at Dundee and make me, as coach of the Coventry Blaze, finish second twice in three competitions the following year was a bitter pill to swallow, but no accident.

Tony spends hours researching players and the league so he gets the right set-up. He is very aware of what is required to run a team, and to take Dundee to the British National League title in his first year and then to runners-up the year after, before taking Edinburgh from seventh to third on a limited budget, really shows it isn't just luck.

Then to take on something that is probably the hardest job in the sport – player/coach at Belfast – and finish top of the scoring charts once again and very nearly pip Coventry to the title, says it all. And this is at an age when some players would be thinking about retirement! Some people would say it is unbelievable. I wouldn't. It shows the talent and dedication Tony possesses.

On the other side of that, unless you get to know him well, and because he has a very professional attitude towards what he does, people do not see his funny side. People close to him will realise that he is the most hysterical man you could ever wish to meet. He is very quick-witted and takes everything in, then comes out with a one-liner that will crease everyone up. He doesn't suffer fools – mentally, he's a tough Scotsman, and that's why he's been at the top since he started playing professionally.

Above all he shows respect. When Dundee beat us in the 2001 BNL Playoff final, there was no gloating like other coaches have done in the past. He just came over to the bench, shook my hand and that was it. He decided that he done what he had to, and didn't feel the need to rub it in. The respect I took from that was immense.

Lots of people talk about what if he would have stayed in America. I see it differently. Yes, he would have been wealthier, but we wouldn't have seen him and ice hockey in the UK would have lost something irrecoverable. Maybe it was supposed to happen.

In a time when the British public and media are crying out for a true sporting hero, they need look no further than Tony Hand MBE. Let's be honest, if he had played football, tennis, rugby or golf he would have gained far more recognition across the sporting world than he has.

To put it into perspective, will Tiger Woods still be winning titles and at the top of his game in twenty-five years? I doubt it. Tony started playing when he was fourteen and is still breaking records today. There is not a sportsman in the world that has dominated his sport as much as Tony Hand has.

And, if he had played football, he would have been multi, multi-millionaire, instead of a multi…

He is the top sportsman of his generation and the greatest ambassador UK hockey has ever had. He has given a lot of people happiness over the years and made a few of his mates very miserable too!

Good luck for the future.

Paul Thompson

Head Coach, Coventry Blaze

FOREWORD BY
GLEN SATHER

Back in 1986, we had a really good scouting system in place and it recommended we take a flyer on Tony Hand. Garry Unger said he would perform well for the Edmonton Oilers. And he did.

The chances of someone really turning out that late in the draft are remote, but this guy had a real chance. It's true that we heard Calgary Flames were interested in Tony, so to take him was nice as it stuck one over them, but if our scouts had him on their list, it would definitely be true that other teams had noticed him too.

We knew it was a long shot but we invited him to one of our training camps and he surprised a lot of people. At the training camp I could see that he had a great ability to read the ice and he was the smartest player there other than Wayne Gretzky. He skated well; his intelligence on the ice really stood out. He was a real prospect.

Tony had an unusual background for someone coming to the NHL to play for one of the best teams around at the time, and he was able to hold his own. He was talented, with a good sense of the game. He had a great attitude and worked really hard. He has great skills with the puck.

I offered him a contract, but he turned me down. I was really disappointed that he didn't accept my deal because he could have advanced in North America. His progress would been celebrated.

I have kept up to date with Tony's progress and I'm glad he has done well. He has worked real hard to get where he is and I like that about him. He's a personable kind of guy too. You always remember those types of players.

I wish him all the luck in the future.

Glen Sather

New York Rangers

1

'SKATING WAS EVERYTHING TO ME...'

'Are you going down the rink?' My eyes rolled. It was a daft question because they both knew I wanted to. I spent my entire life down there. Seven days a week skating, gliding across the ice, flying around, practising – it was my life.

Along with my brothers Paul and David, I used to head down to Murrayfield Ice Rink in Edinburgh all the time. I was ten, Paul two years older, David three years younger and we all used to hang around in a big group with people like Scott Neil, Ronnie Wood and Moray Hanson.

My dad died of a heart attack when I was seven so I always looked up to my brothers as well as the other guys there and they took good care of me. Everyone looked after each other because they had to, and only having my mother at home meant everyone kept an eye on me.

It would take us a good hour and a half to get to the rink and at first we used to catch two buses. But after a while we decided to walk down with that group of friends. It saved us a few quid so we could afford to skate. The rink must have been a good six miles from our house in Muirhouse, but we didn't think about it.

It's fair to say that where I lived wasn't great. It was a rough council estate, with no drugs, unlike today, but we just wanted to get away as much as we could. We went to the rink because everyone enjoyed going there and I really did grow up with skates attached to my feet.

Looking back, I wouldn't have changed it for anything. Skating was everything to me. The social scene was great, as there was a great crowd down there as well as some real characters. There was an old guy called Jimmy who used to mime to songs on the balcony over-looking the rink and no one paid him any attention! We also knew it was skating time when 'War of the Worlds' came over the PA system. But I just wanted to be better. I spent as much time down on the ice as I could to skate quicker and to be able to move backwards and make sharp turns. I loved it. I darted in and out of everyone with the bigger kids trying to catch me! I wasn't a slight kid by any means – my family were quite 'thick' and pretty solid – but I became very strong on my feet. And whenever I could get hold of a hockey stick I used to practise hitting the puck and tapping it around.

I always borrowed sticks, and loved using them, but after a while I wanted one of my own. In those days they were really expensive and my mum couldn't afford to buy me one, so I saved my money for ages and managed to scrape enough together to buy a KOHO 2210. It was one I had used to practise with and happened to be quite affordable too. Unfortunately, it weighed a ton and was the size of a two-by-four plank of wood. I bought it from Richard Stirling, who looked after the juniors at the rink, for the princely sum of £3, which was a lot of money then. Those sticks never used to break, unlike the ones day today. And you didn't want to break it either, not at that price! I guarded it with my life.

After a while, I was fortunate enough that Mr Willie Kerr, the nice 'old man' who owned the rink, noticed I spent a lot of time there and gave me some work. He was great. As long as you put in the time, he would let you go on the ice, even when it was shut.

I must have done everything down there at some point. I handed out the skates, cleaned the floors, collected tickets and drove the Zamboni. It may have only been a few quid at the end of the week, but it was worth it because I loved the place.

By the age of fourteen, as well as working many hours at the rink, I was playing for Murrayfield's junior team, the Raiders, having moved up from the Ravens. At the end of each public session when I had tidied up, I used to hang around and watch the Murrayfield Racers play. They were quick and strong and I longed to play alongside the amazing guys on that team like Alex Dampier and Chris Kelland.

They came in as University players and although they dominated for a while before more Uni and NHL-based players joined the league, they really set the trend. Everyone thought they were the greatest and they really changed the style of how hockey could be played. They did amazing things and were very strong.

Working and playing at the rink meant I could rub shoulders with these guys and I often sat on the bench handing out their sticks. The guys were great with me and Alex was superb. He bought me my first pair of plastic boots and I have never looked back since. Players these days give me a bit of ribbing about my boots, but I'm a simple man; I like them comfortable and easy to use. Plastic boots are simple and easy! You just give them a bit of oil now and again and they are fine. As there are only so many made in size eight, I try and get hold of as many pairs as I can. Money was tight back then so you just needed a pair of boots that could do the job. Plastic ones lasted a lot longer than others. The ice was also a lot 'wetter' back then, so they stood up to the water better.

Anyway, I digress. Apart from changing my views on skates, Alex also had faith in my abilities and took me to a hockey school in his home town of Thunder Bay, Canada when I was fifteen. He really helped me along and showed me what ice hockey was all about – I will never forget him for this. The camp was at an 'elite' level and he believed that by getting me used to North American ice hockey I would be ready if I ever went over there. It was a great experience and I also won the top player award.

He told me a story recently that when I was on the ice he would sit with a load of scouts. One time they were chatting and one of the scouts said to him, 'Look at that Swedish kid. Boy, can he skate.' Alex said I wasn't Swedish but a Scot and then had to explain that we did play hockey over here!

Alex spent a few years in Edinburgh, where he coached, and I later met up with him again at the Sheffield Steelers. With Alex you always got honesty. He had the ability to be straightforward when he wanted to be. He was a good guy and certainly helped me along in my career.

You could say Murrayfield was my 'real' home. I was skating on Monday, Wednesday and Friday evenings and then practising with the Raiders on Saturdays – with public sessions before and after, then back at the rink on Sunday afternoon. My friends and I then used to get the rink ready for the Racers' main game.

The skating did me the world of good and I was lucky enough to represent Great Britain in Pool C of the European Junior Championships, and took the leading points scorer award with 10 points from 4 games. It was a five-day tournament held at Billingham in March 1982 and the team did well, playing Hungary and Spain, winning one (Spain 5-4), drawing one (Hungary 6-6) and losing two (Hungary 8-4, Spain 6-5) to take the bronze medal. Great Britain had players like Stephen Cooper, my brother Paul and Moray Hanson in its roster and other really talented kids like Hugh Findlay, but some didn't make it and quit playing before their time.

The GB juniors were a skilful team coached by Racers' player Lawrie Lovell and managed by Hall of Famer John Rost. We used to train in Billingham on a Friday night, which meant getting picked up and then being dropped off really late. On the Saturday, I would be back at the rink, working and skating! Although I must have spent most of the time tired, I didn't care. Hockey was something I loved.

Getting the medal and award were my first serious 'titles' and I would always look back on these throughout my career. They gave me the springboard to show I could compete, but little did I know that, six months later, my life would change.

2

'A REAL DREAM COME TRUE...'

Murrayfield Racers were one of those clubs that will always be synonymous with tradition, history and, above all, winning. They had dominated all league and cup competitions at the back end of the seventies and, going into the next decade, looked very strong. They always had close battles with Fife Flyers and Durham Wasps and the rinks would regularly be packed out to watch these contests. The team had some great players back then, such as Duncan McIntyre and my cousin Scott Neil, and they were part of the Racers' success.

When I retire from playing, I will always look back fondly at the goals and points I scored in internationals, Wembley finals and tight games, but those early days and close rivalries also remain a real career highlight for me. Watching from the stands I could see how the players and fans reacted to a great move, goal, hit, fight or moment.

I first got my chance to sample a bit of that when I made my senior debut for the Racers on 20 September 1981, against the Flyers in the Northern League and Scottish League. I was just fourteen and up against these big fellas who wanted to see what I was all about. It was difficult to know how to play these guys, but I just wanted to play my game – even though I didn't know I had one at the time. Don't get me wrong, I knew I had a talent, but I also knew that I had practised and worked hard for it. All the hours at the rink were paying off and it was real fun.

Why did I get a break? Because the Racers had some very good GB players on the roster. They used to head off around the world with the national team. Over the next few weeks I gained more and more shifts and increased my ice time. Getting a break so young was amazing, especially with several imports coming in. But the league was running at only three imports per team, so British players were crucial to success. because most of the team were amateur, we loat players all the time but we still had to play the games and I had to make up the numbers. Netminder Moray Hanson was also 'called up'.

On 17 October 1981 we had to play the Billingham Bombers because of such a player shortage. Of course this was nothing special, but the game will long live in the memory. Even though we were shorthanded, I had to wait fifteen minutes to get on the ice. I knew I would feature eventually but it was agonising waiting for the chance. Finally, I was asked to make up a forward line with Lawrie Lovell and Chris Kelland. Alex Dampier just told me to go and play my game.

As I skated on, I didn't feel nervous to be honest, just excited. Then, the face-off went our way and I picked up the puck and managed to slide a pass into Kelland. Cool as you like, he slotted it home. My first point. Kelland assisted by no.9, Tony Hand. It was an amazing feeling to gain it, but I didn't think anything of it at the time. I was doing my job and the team had scored. I just wanted to look like I knew what I was doing! It was very frightening being a little boy with all those massive fellas.

On that day I wore the no.9 shirt and I have always tried to wear it since. I took over that number from Willie Kerr, who was the son of Willie who owned the rink. In fact, the Kerrs are still the venue's major shareholders. Willie was one of the premier players in Edinburgh at the time so it was a real honour.

It took another month (15 November) before I gained my first goal – in my eighth game for the team. Again we were short-benched on a road trip to Durham Wasps in the Northern League and I took a nice pass from my boyhood hero Derek 'Pecker' Reilly to score at 8.55. I then added a second in the third as we ran away with it 16-5. It was a real dream come true for me. These guys were real stars and having watched them from the stands, I was now playing alongside them. In 19 games that 1981/82 season I scored 4 times, with 7 assists, taking 12 penalties in minutes.

Up until then, there had never been any hint of an ice hockey legacy in my family. I was born in Edinburgh on 15 August 1967, the second-born to Lorraine and David Hand, and had a pretty normal upbringing. Losing my dad was obviously hard for all of us to take, but we were close-knit as a family and really pulled together. I went to St Augustine's Catholic School but never had what you would class as a true Catholic upbringing. My mum always used to encourage me and my brothers to go to church, but we didn't want to. She still does to this day! Paul, like me, had always wanted to play for the Racers.

Although I was still at school I was playing hockey and skating as much as I could. It's fair to say that, back then, school didn't matter that much. That may make me sound like I was a dummy; not true; I did okay at school, but the pressure to do well wasn't really on you. It's true that I must have been knackered all the time from playing with the Racers and Raiders and working in the rink, but I didn't think about it. It was real fun. I often wonder what my mum must have thought as I dragged myself off to the rink at the weekend, played a game, walked back and then went to school the next morning. Then again, with three boys in the house, she was probably glad of the peace. If only she knew I used to get my head down on the bus to school as well.

Life was a bit weird when I broke into the team. I had camera crews coming to the house, especially when I started making headlines, but in my eyes I hadn't really done anything. I was always quite focused mentally, but all I ever wanted to do was to play professionally for the Racers and I never dreamed it would go this far.

Turning fifteen in August, I knew that I was going to get a few more games for the Racers, but never expected to feature as much as I did. That season (1982/83) I scored 42 points in 24 games, including a four-goal game against Whitley Warriors in December in the British League Section A. Coached by Lawrie Lovell, the team again did well but never finished the job it began. The Racers finished second in the league but Dundee beat us 12-9 on aggregate in the Heineken British Championships Scottish Finals; we won 8-7 at their place but then crumbled 1-5 at home

I also played in Pool C at the European Junior Championships in Sarajevo in the former Yugoslavia. We finished second in the group, beating Belgium 7-1, drawing against Spain and losing 7-4 to the hosts. I came away with five points. The Olympics were due to be held around then and they used us as practice. We had a police escort everywhere and it was an eye-opening experience.

As I played more and more I could feel myself getting stronger and I could also see that the opposition were started to get a little less friendly with me on the ice too. Entertaining? You bet. I wouldn't class myself as being a dirty player back then, even now, but there were plenty of arseholes trying to wind you up. I've had this all my career, but being so young meant that they really wanted to test you. You had to drop the gloves quite a lot to gain respect, otherwise you would be targeted in later games.

I never in my whole career tried to cheap shot someone or injure them. You had to look after yourself and not be afraid to throw a hit. I was never a tough player, but I also didn't want anyone to look after me. I saw that as the only way to gain respect. I did have players who wanted to help me out and it is always good to have someone backing you up – but I wanted a go first!

When you're that age you are trying to impress and enjoy yourself. When you look back at sportspeople through the years, the ones that have proved themselves time and time again are the people that wanted it when they were young. You have to want it at nine and ten years old and perhaps even younger. If not, it's half-hearted. This is not something you can teach, you have to want it. And that's not just in sport; in any field you have to want to do something to succeed.

I never went in expecting to be a professional hockey player, and let's be honest, it's not something I ever expected to make stacks of money out of either (not that I have; you can make decent money, but nothing you can retire on). Hockey is something that's in your blood. In those days no one was really making a living out of the sport – bar the imports. They were given a house and car and you did think they were on a fortune. Chris Kelland and Alex Dampier were really the first guys to make money. But as Heineken got involved and then Smirnoff sponsored the Racers, plus the television coverage, the owners started to pay the players more than just expenses. Of course, at fifteen I wasn't making a great deal and, to be honest, I didn't care. Money has never been an issue with me.

Unfortunately, just before the new season when I was away at the hockey school and staying with Alex Dampier, Murrayfield lost its 'old man'. Willie Kerr, who I owe so much as he helped pay for me to go over to the hockey school, died in August while he was on duty in the rink. He was seventy-two. Although Alex had suggested taking me over to Canada it was Willie who wanted me to continue improving and helped me out. He was a great man. You sometimes forget about people who put you on the road when you are young, but if he had never sent me to Canada or let me skate and work at the rink as much as he had, then who knows? I am really grateful for him and his sons Ian and Chalky (Willie) for what they did for me. I am very proud to have known these people and glad that the rink is still in their name.

By the latter end of 1983, just after I turned sixteen, I felt like I wanted to give the sport more of my time. All the way through the summer I was skating non-stop and I had grown up a lot in the five months since the end of the season. The Canada trip was superb, I worked hard in public sessions, scrimmaged and played with friends all the time. Everything was right. Coach Alex Dampier was encouraging me and I was in the right environment.

That season I just flew. Murrayfield did relatively well that year, making the playoff final and finishing fifth in the Heineken Premiership. The final was fantastic but the Dundee Rockets were just too strong, beating us 5-4. They had players like Roy Halpin (175 points), Ronnie Wood, (119), Alistair Wood (58) and Jim Pennycook on their roster.

I played something like 40 games that year and I was still at school! But when you are young, you find the energy, especially if it is something you love doing. I finished the league campaign just 5 short of 100 points, with 52 goals and 43 assists. In 7 games of the Autumn Cup I rattled up 20 points and the playoffs brought 15 points. The team back then were superb and we all just clicked, even though we didn't win anything 'major'. I was top scorer, with Jim Lynch, John Hay and Bill Sobkowich grabbing 170 points between them. My brother finished leading penalty taker out of all the team and Paul Heavey wasn't afraid to throw them about either. I also represented Great Britain at the World Junior Championships, scoring 9 points from 4 games.

I made great progress in my game that year, but cannot put my finger on why. Edinburgh was a big ice rink and that meant I could develop my positioning and see things better. Even then, I considered myself a playmaker. Although I was learning about the game, if I had the puck I always knew who was coming up in front of me and behind. It's something I have always prided myself on. I can adjust my speed and know exactly where to go to get a guy in position on the ice. It is a real numbers game. You are always looking and evaluating the play. If there is a guy behind me falling down and he was supposed to be backchecking, you know in about five seconds you are able to outnumber the team inside his own blueline. Then it is a case of finding the player that can set it all up, fire a shot or create a further play. It's all done in the blink of an eye. I know if someone is caught behind the net, or is caught in the corner in our end, that if I get the puck high I will be able to find someone. It is all about timing.

Back then there were players that wanted to get to the net as quickly as they could, but I never saw that as being the best strategy. You needed to know what is happening, who is in position and have the ability to make the passes at speed, controlling your skating. I still do this now, even though my skating has slowed doen. When I was young I was trying hard to develop this skill. I also wanted to know who was on the same line as me because if I passed to them I needed to know what foot they shot off and if they liked it between their skates.

At the end of the season I only had a few months left at school, and lined myself up an apprenticeship as a thermal engineer at Mossmorran, a local chemical plant.

3

'WE SHOWED WHAT WAS APPLE SAUCE TO THE DOCTOR...'

After the amazing year the Racers had, we wanted to build going into the 1984/85 season. I just wanted to keep on playing.

Although I was only seventeen, my 100th league goal came against Durham in December as part of a hat-trick and I also guested for Dundee in the European Cup, scoring twice. To think these days that you could play for another club while contracted to another would make people laugh, but it happened in those days.

I was on a line with Jim Lynch and Jock (John) Hay. Jimmy went on to coach Ayr and Fife and was a real good guy. One of the premier players at the time, he never skated really well, but he was an amazing passer. Jock complimented him well as he was a great skater with amazing vision. In that team we also had a pretty good back line too, with Paul Heavey and my brother Paul on the D.

Those guys meant I could get forward and convert the chances they sent my way. In 36 league games I scored 72 goals with 92 assists for 164 points. I also scored a further 51 points in the cup and play-offs. That assist total broke the record held by Roy Halpin of the Dundee Rockets. The team was also really intense. I have always loved playing with teams like that – with guys that really care. Some can go from season to season just doing the job, but those players at Murrayfield wanted to win.

With a young team we hung on during the year and managed to finish third in the league behind Durham and Fife, have a decent run in the Autumn Cup and make the playoff finals at Wembley. In between, I represented Great Britain at the European Junior Championships (Pool C) in Feltre, Italy. We played Italy and Belgium but just couldn't match the intensity of our competitors. Because things were pretty hectic back home in terms of fixtures and sponsors' requests, I was allowed to play as long as I missed the last match to get home and compete in a league game. We won one game against Italy 8-5 and I finished with 4 points from 3 games.

A month earlier I had been denied the chance to play in the World Juniors in Belgium because Smirnoff insisted I play in the televised league game against Durham along with Alex Dampier, my brother Paul and Lindsay Lovell. The BIHA did offer to fly us back from Belgium but Murrayfield declined.

Once again, Wembley proved to be our downfall. We hammered Ayr in the semis but for the second year in a row we lost – this time 9-4. Dave Stoyanovich inspired Fife that year, but the team was jammed full of imported talent and really tough British guys. Ron Plumb was somebody everyone looked at. He was thirty-five, had had a great career in the States and had been drafted for Boston Bruins.

Defeats are always hard to take, and this was my second in a play-off final. But being young, it really was just another game. I took it in my stride, and never got carried away. We were up for it, but we didn't have our best game and Fife capitalised on that and played too well for us. Dave got a hat-trick in that game, which really pissed Heavey off. At the end of the third period, he went after Stoyanovich because he was 'upset' that that he was scoring so many. He certainly gave him a few licks, but nothing too serious.

I always look back on those Wembley days and feel that the sport lost something when the playoff weekend moved to other venues. I understand that the reasoning behind it was financial. Why go and rent a rink that was costing more than £100,000? To be fair, it wasn't a great facility for the players, but great for the fans. To pay that much money for those games was extortionate, but when you have a facility like Nottingham with a home hockey team, it is better to keep the money in your own back garden.

These days, Nottingham do put on a good show at the National Ice Centre, but Wembley just had that special something. You played the games in a truly loud and amazing atmosphere. The hotel was up the road and the fans used to congregate and sing outside. Flying was also a big thing back then and the fans and players would come down by plane. It was a big event.

And the sponsors were great. Smirnoff was Murrayfield's principal sponsor and they laid on the flights. League and Championship (playoff) sponsors Heineken used to put up a marquee for the players after the games so we could socialise – it was like: the season was over, the curtain was down. I can't imagine that ever happening in any other sport. Nowadays, I may be a little old fashioned, but it is like: 'the season is over – see ya's!' It seems like they want you to play the game and get you out as quick as possible.

The good thing about hockey players is that ninety-five per cent are down-to-earth, good guys. Don't get me wrong, there are some wankers who think they are something special – you always get players who think they are great and are doing teams a favour by playing for them. But the real hockey players are fantastic – most have got to where they are the hard way. I am friends with a lot of guys from other teams and while everyone is desperate to win, when the game is over… it's over. I've seen guys knock lumps out of each other and scrap all the time during a game and then enjoy a pint together afterwards.

Wembley was a 'full on' weekend. Every team tried to gain an advantage over its rivals. One time we had oxygen on the bench because it was so hot, even though we didn't have a clue how to use it. Some guys were taking ginseng to give them a boost – but all it did was cost them a few quid. One time we ate baby food to increase our energy, because babies are full of energy aren't they? We showed what was apple sauce to the doctor and asked him if it was any good. He looked up and he said: 'Yes, with pork!' We really did not know what we were doing. In the end, despite how nice it tasted, medical science proved us wrong, But then again, it wasn't difficult...

Was Wembley all sweetness and nice? Well, partly. I actually always thought Wembley was a little unfair. You always played two games over the weekend, but due to television coverage you could play late on Saturday and then the final on Sunday. Your opponents could be sat in the hotel eating and socialising and you could be halfway through the second period! Getting six hours' extra rest could mean all the difference.

The thing about the playoffs is that they are 'no holds barred'. All the players want to win and are very pumped up. It's human nature. If you play in mid-November and the season is halfway though with 40 games to go, you cannot be as pumped up. Everyone gives everything... even the coach, the fans and the organisation, are all up for it. You don't want to get knocked out. If you win you get five months to celebrate; lose and it's five months' thinking time. It's that clear cut.

To lose that final against Fife was hard. We all felt like shit. But deep down we knew that we were young, the talent was there and that we would eventually win it. We had to bounce back straight away and we did the season after. At no point did I think that we would be runners-up again. I have never gone through my career fearing the worst. Of course, I am more realistic now! I'm not so stupid to think that if one team spends double what the other does, they don't have an advantage. It is obviously twice as hard to compete. But in those days there was a level playing field. Even though there was no salary cap, all the teams really did spend the same give or take a few notes. In Edinburgh, we had a good team. There was me, Moray Hanson, Paul Hand, Paul Pentland, Paul Heavey, Scott Neil and Chris Kelland and with some additions I always felt we would win something.

Before the 1985/86 season started we recruited Rick Fera from Kingston Canadians. Rick was a 'junior B' player from the States and the British game really suited him. He had an amazing talent around the net. In those days if you signed a 'junior A' player, you were getting a superstar. We did have some doubts about him coming over here, but he certainly showed us his worth. He was a real character and his philosophy was 'way out there' but he was a good guy, if a little different. It was a real surprise how we clicked but we had a great chemistry together and it worked. Some guys don't have the ability to think as part of a team, they think as individuals, but we really hit it off. Rick scored 110 goals that year, with 86 assists and I had my best year to date – 164 points in the league (79 goals, 85 assists), and 71 points in the cup and play-offs. My 200th goal came in my 128th league game (8 February 1986), against the Peterborough Pirates, when I scored four.

As our partnership developed so did the team. We kept hold of our players and we all matured together. Scott Neil had a great season. He always had a good eye for net and he worked hard and did well for the team. My brother and Paul Heavey carried on where they left off the previous year by holding together our defence. They were always rucking and the fans loved it. There was none of today's 'third man in' and it was never bad, but everyone loved to play and the passions came out. Okay, it didn't help matters that they both played on the same line and amassed 245 penalty minutes between them, but it was a real revered line. While we are chatting about fighting, a quick point – I have never seen a stage-managed fight, only a few guys come out with sore faces!

It was that consistent roster that proved to be the key that year. We kept a strong nucleus of good guys and we always knew that whoever was on the ice, their heart and soul was in the team. That year, we lost the final of the Scottish Cup 7-3 against Dundee and finished behind Durham Wasps in the League. In between we picked off Durham in the Norwich Union (Autumn) Cup 8-5 and avenged the defeat to Dundee in the playoffs.

I also played in Pool C at the World Junior Championships in France, which was a cracking experience. We took the bronze medal just behind the hosts and Denmark to gain our best result to date. I scored ten goals as the team really clicked, but we couldn't match the top two teams. Incidentally, we lost to France 14-2 in a game that included ten powerplay goals from the French team!

We were on a roll that year and Murrayfield's 2,000-plus crowds certainly helped. We fed off them and sold out on a number of occasions. The supporters propelled us to Wembley and were superb as we won 4-2. We had already beaten Ayr 8-4 in the semis with five goals, including two shorties, from myself, but Dundee headed into that game as favourites, with netminder Martin McKay, Roch Bois and NHLer Garry Unger as well as Ronnie and Ali Wood in their line-up, but we got on top of them and never let go. They scored first through Unger, but Fera equalised before Scott Neil put us ahead early in the second period. Bois levelled it up once again in the third but we went ahead twenty-eight seconds later and never looked back. And yes, the following five months of celebrating were superb!

Looking back, the partnership with Rick certainly helped me develop as a player, but the rest of the team was good and so I was noticed. The top scorer in a bad team is never noticed. If you're in a good team and you're winning, it's easier to get recognition.

At the playoffs I was presented with the Young Player of the Year award, which capped one of the most amazing days of my life. We used to get a hat from Vic Batchelder of *Ice Hockey News Review* magazine if we were judged Young Player of the Month and I had won it twice so I knew I was in with a shout.

Part of the prize was to spend a couple of weeks at the Calgary Flames training camp, which Vic had arranged with the Canadian province of Alberta. The idea was to go to the camp and train with the best NHL players. You were never going to make the team; it was like winning the lottery or something – a real prize. I spent all summer looking forward to it, but fate always has a nasty way of changing things...

4

'FROM BEHIND THE HAGGIS CURTAIN...'

I had waited a good four weeks for the details of the Calgary training camp to emerge when one day the phone rang. I picked it up and a Canadian voice at the other end congratulated me and asked how I felt about icing in Edmonton. It was a very strange thing to come out with so I nervously laughed and said, 'No, I'm on my way to the Flames.'

After a short silence the guy said he was from a radio station in Canada, said I had been drafted and would be heading to the Oilers. To be honest I had no idea how the draft worked and thought it was a cast-iron wind-up anyway (and an unfunny one at that), so I pleaded innocence and said I was looking forward to training in Calgary.

But he just laughed and that was that! Putting the phone down I was a little bemused with what had just happened. I obviously knew who Edmonton were – anyone who knows anything about hockey knows the Oilers were probably the best team ever and were creating a dynasty that would see them win five Stanley Cups in the 1980s. Under coach Glen Sather, the Oilers had beaten the NY Islanders four games to one to win the cup in 1984 and beat Philadelphia by the same scoreline a year later. Later, in 1987, they won emerged victorious over Philadelphia again and then whitewashed Boston a year later.

But I thought I had won a chance to train at Calgary and that was it for me. I didn't give the call a second thought and continued to think about what the Calgary camp would be like.

A few days later I got a call from the chief scout at Edmonton, a chap called Barry Fraiser. Now, this chat certainly made things a lot clearer. He was straight upfront saying I had been drafted by Edmonton and that come September I would be training with them. Apparently once you are drafted, if you go to America to play or train for a NHL team, the 'drafting' team holds your rights for two years.

I was gobsmacked. Winning the Young Player of the Year award was amazing, getting a place with Calgary was something else, but being drafted by the best team in the world... no way! The idea behind the draft is to make sure that the talent gets evenly spread around the teams in the league. If you finish bottom of the NHL, you will get the first and normally the best player around. It gives the 'lower' clubs a chance to be better. Then, the further up the league you go, the 'lower' the class of drafted talent.

It is a complicated system. Teams can trade their draft pick numbers to other NHL clubs throughout the season and can effectively scout what players they want. It turned out that Garry Unger – an amazing ex-NHL player who had played for Dundee among others in the UK – was doing some part-time scouting work for the Oilers and had recommended me to Barry. He had played against me a few times and had reported back to Glen and they had decided to take a punt on me. To be fair, I still thought it was all a bit strange – why would they want a nineteen-year-old from Scotland? – but I was sure as hell going to make the best of it.

It was very daunting. I would be training alongside the likes of Wayne Gretzky – the greatest player ever – and Mark Messier, who scored 1,887 regular-season points in 1,756 games. I certainly had the right to feel it was a bit of a wind-up. Edmonton and Calgary were bitter rivals at the time. They had fought tooth and nail for the title and never really got on. In fact, I'm sure they got great delight out of putting one over on each other. For Edmonton to snatch me from Calgary's training camp; people said it was to piss the Flames off.

Funnily enough, Glen Sather admitted as much later, as he said it was nice to do that and would have done so at any given opportunity! But my drafting was serious. Glen was pleased with Garry and Barry's recommendation and wanted to see what I could do. He also later said that there were other teams looking at drafting me.

As the summer went on, it started to dawn on me that I was going to Edmonton. Why it had taken a while for me to realise, I don't know, but I was young and very excited. Of course, I could have turned it all down and stayed in Scotland, but that would have been pure madness. I had to give it my best shot.

It turned out that the press in Calgary were giving it their best shot too! Understandably, they saw this situation as one-upmanship from their closest rivals. Headlines such as 'From Behind the Haggis Curtain' appeared in papers and they took great delight in poking fun at Edmonton's twelfth-round, #252 draft pick. They thought that the Oilers were making a mockery of the draft because there was no way that a young Scot could make it in that league. Add to that the fact that I was supposed to be over in Calgary and the conspiracy theorists may have had a point.

I was stuck in the middle of all this but I've never really given a second thought to my coverage in the papers so it all flew over me. Yes I was the last pick of the last round. The 'joke' pick almost, but I was determined to make the best of it.

5

'I KNEW I WAS HOLDING MY OWN...'

Before I headed over to Edmonton I met up with Fraser McColl, the uncle of one of the owners of Stagecoach, the bus company. He was a proper, straightforward Scot who must have been worth millions of pounds. He owned the WHL-based Victoria Cougars and said to me in a hotel next to Murrayfield that if the camp didn't go well, I could stay over there and play with his team. He also said I could train with them beforehand to get myself ready. Of course I said yes and headed over there in early September to work on my skills and fitness.

When the camp came around, I wasn't nervous and really looked forward to the experience. I felt I had nothing to lose because I knew that I probably wouldn't be picked for the team anyway. For me to get in that side I would have had to oust players like Gretzky, Messier and Jari Kurri – real legends with more Stanley Cup Rings than fingers. Let's just say that reality set in! But I knew I was really lucky. The kudos of icing for the Oilers would be terrific.

After arriving in Edmonton I was picked up from the airport and put up in a nice hotel next to the rink. My roommate was second-round pick Jamie Nicolls, a strong skater who had come from the WHL's Portland Winter Hawks. We chatted a lot about what the camp was like but you never really had a chance to socialise. The camps are about winning and training. Of the fifty-five people who turned up at the camp, there were

35

guys that had contracts with the Oilers, Edmonton's farm team and the rest who were looking for a job. All the guys wanted to win a contract and it was fiercely competitive, but great fun too! I met some great people there and some, such as Tim Salmon, Mike Ware (who had been drafted the year before), Ivan Matulik, who came from behind the Iron Curtain and so had a lot of press coverage, and Darren Durdle, are still friends to this day.

When you look back at that draft, Edmonton took a look at some really decent players but not many actually made it in the NHL. Their first-round pick, Kim Issel played just four games at the top level. Jamie didn't make it. Ron Shudra carved out a good career in the UK. Dan Currie (fourth round) made 22 appearances and Davud Haas (fifth) made seven. Draft picks really are hit and miss.

At the camp, the idea was to train in the morning, go through drills and other tests and then play a game in the evening. You would be being watched all the time by scouts and everyone wanted to do well. There would be regular fights on the ice so players could show who was the toughest. It lasted two weeks, but they cut people every day that didn't make the grade. I lasted the full fourteen days and finished as one of the top scorers. I didn't think I stood out, but I knew I held my own.

It took me a while to realise that players were leaving us all the time. After a week I noticed that the camp was smaller and worked out what was going on! I really did think that some had decided to go home or were training at different times. When you're nineteen and have never been in that situation it is difficult to comprehend these things.

Some of the guys there had around ten sticks to their names. I only took one over with me, a KOHO 2210, which was supposed to be unbreakable. Of course, I broke it on my first day and had to borrow one of Marty McSorley's. I got a fair amount of stick from the trainers because I only owned one.

One of the first tests they put me through was a fitness check. I had been playing for one of the best sides in Scotland, skating all the time, so I expected to breeze through it. It is amazing how wrong you can be. My results, in my view, were nothing short of horrendous! Yes, I was in good shape, but I wasn't strong enough. It really did show how much we were in the dark ages back home. Other people at the camp had trained very hard to be there and were very fit whereas I had been skating at the rink, lifting a few weights and scrimmaging with my friends!

I was 165 lbs at the time, but some of the players had bulked up to 190. Some were 220. I wasn't going over as a tough guy however – rather as a finesse player – but I really had to work hard. My flexibility test was one of the best at the whole camp. My suppleness, however, couldn't stop 6ft 3in and 230 lbs of player shoving me off the puck and straining my back: I went in to grab the puck from Dave Semenko, but he just put an arm out and completely flattened me. It was a clean hit and what you would class as a friendly 'shove off' which sent me flying. My back started to spasm and I had to take a day out.

Apart from that, the camp was fantastic. Everyone encouraged each other and the younger lads like myself and Ivan Matulik had the NHL players spurring us on. Playing with those guys really opened my eyes about the sport. Of course, one of the main highlights was playing alongside Wayne Gretzky. Wayne was, and still is, the biggest name in the sport. He is a true legend. He finished his career with 3,239 points and even to be in the same room as him was a dream come true. I have to admit that I hardly spoke to him! Let's just say that a nineteen-year-old's nerves got the better of me.

One time I was being interviewed by a posse of reporters outside the locker room and Wayne walked past and looked up as if to say 'who the hell is this person with all these around him?' – he looked really surprised. As a player he was immense. He used to talk to the guys in the dressing room and gave them loads of encouragement. I watched him do this and admired the time he had for people. I really looked up to him.

Mark Messier was also an amazing player. I played on a line with him at the camp and he would talk all the time and give you loads of encouragement. I took the puck off him once and skated through to score and he was really humble. As I turned around, he skated over and said, 'Well done Tony,' though gritted teeth! Being so young and Scottish brought me loads of attention but everyone was fine with me all the time. At that level of hockey you need to treat everyone the same, as you never know – some players can slip through the net.

But it was unusual for someone who learnt the trade in Scotland to be at a NHL training camp. Back home everyone was really excited but I never once felt any weight of pressure on me. I had to be focused all the time so I could match the level expected of me.

At the end of the camp I was called into Glen Sather's office for 'negotiation'. Well… it is supposed to be a discussion but I was never in a position to bargain. Here was a young Scot going into the office of the most successful general manager in North America at the time, looking for a contract! Glen was sitting there in a massive chair with a cigar in one hand and I thought, 'You are kidding, right? What do I say here?' He said he was impressed with how I had played and offered me a contract to play 'junior' for a year. He also said I had surprised a few people with how I turned out.

But I was pretty homesick by then, having been away for three months, so I asked what would happen if I decided to go home. Glen really understood and said that it was fine. He said I had done really well and playing back at home would not damage my development in any way, but he wanted me to come back in a year. This was great for me as I fancied coming back and training again, so I accepted.

After the camp I was knackered but decided to take up Fraser's offer and ice with Victoria. My thinking was to stay over there and play with the team before returning to Edmonton the year after to take part in another camp. The offer was there and despite my home-sickness I thought it was worth a try.

I played 3 games for the Cougars and scored 8 points but something wasn't right so I decided to come home. Don't get me wrong, Victoria was good and the WHL was clearly a step up from the level in Britain, but I just didn't feel comfortable there. I had never experienced anything like that before and my body couldn't cope. I was constantly being questioned by the press, playing and training and when I got home I just had no energy to do anything. My local doctor said it was too much because I was young and I needed to rest.

When I returned to Murrayfield it was buzzing. Everyone wanted to talk to me and there were a lot of clubs, such as Nottingham, battling for my signature. But I only ever wanted to play in Edinburgh and that was confirmed when it was announced that they held my rights so I had no choice! I had never signed a contract, so why this was the case I didn't really understand. Back then, if a team gave you two sticks you were classed as their player. But I was more than happy to return. This was pre-Bosman so I suppose you could say that players had less power than they do now. Now you would just laugh if a team tried to do this. It was never an issue, but it would have been nice to be given a choice! Really I had no intention of heading elsewhere. Edinburgh was a good place to play and I really enjoyed it.

6

'IT DIDN'T FEEL RIGHT AND THAT WAS MY DECISION…'

After being told by my doctor to takes things easy, it took me around five minutes to ignore that advice and go straight back into the thick of the action. Being back home gave me a new bout of energy and all I wanted to do was hit the ice again.

It's fair to say that I came back from the camp with a swagger in my step, because I had been up there and trained with the best. This may sound arrogant; in reality it was far from it. I have always been one of those people who likes to keep their feet on the ground. There's an old saying: don't ride your highs high and your lows low – otherwise you'll be up and down all the time.

I have never been the sort of person that gets overexcited about what I have achieved, because in sport you are always going to have low times. By adopting this approach it means I can take the barren spells in my stride and not think about what happened last week or last year. It also gives me the drive to continue succeeding. There have been people who have played amazingly well for a season only to fall away the year after. Sport is fickle, so I try not to get too excited. Of course, I like to do well and I like my teams to do well, but I have never bragged about what I have done.

When I came back people wanted to talk to me and plenty of teams wanted my signature but I just wanted to play. In my life I have never chased the money – my first professional contract was for £40 a week. Okay, it's supply and demand; if you're at the top of your game you expect to be paid a decent wage. I was fully professional at this time, and might have secured some decent money if I would have moved, but Edinburgh was my home and I loved it there. In any case, I was up against two of the tightest Scotsmen in the world. Billy Dunbar and Richard Stirling who managed the club were renowned for having short arms and deep pockets! You could never get any money out of those two.

There have certainly been some average players over the years take good money and take money away from the sport as a result. But that isn't the players' fault; it is the owners' for not doing their scouting and research well enough. Back in those days you would have four guys in a team that were on top money. Around 1986/87, a University player such as Dundee's Chris Brinster would be classed as a top earner. Some clubs looked to compete with the likes of these guys by signing junior B players from Canada to fill the gap – but they just weren't up to the burgeoning league at that time. These days it's the NHL guys that are the top earners in clubs.

I know I sound like an old man, but when I negotiate with players these days the first thing they want to know is how much money they will make. Back in those days I just wanted to play and the cash was a bonus. They don't seem to care if they will be playing as long as they are earning something like a decent wage. And this is even before they make the grade. They want the money but they don't want any shit you may give them. They seem not to want to take a professional attitude. Perhaps it's just the way sport is and younger players believe they can make some serious money out of hockey. But clubs have to try and develop these players as well as attracting quality talent so they can compete.

Back in Murrayfield, when I returned from the camp, we had a talented team, but also one where the players wanted to play for each other. Again we had retained much of the Championship-winning roster and we had acquired people like Brian Burley and Ian

Ramsay, as well as Stevie Coombe who had stepped up from the juniors, so we were hopeful for the season. In those days rosters had a tendency to stay the same, as no one really travelled a lot. There was a real rivalry in the league and you certainly wouldn't move to your local rivals. Of course, that happens all the time now, but back then you wouldn't dream of playing for Fife when you played for Murrayfield!

Fife did offer me a serious amount of money a few years later to move, but it didn't feel right at the time. Fife was a great organisation with a fanatical set of supporters, but I loved the Racers and wanted to stay. They tapped me up again in 1995 when the then Edinburgh Racers went under, but I moved to Sheffield instead. While we are on the subject, Cardiff also offered me amazing money one year – something like £1,000 a week! I think if I had taken the money I would have been a millionaire by now! Johnny Lawless was flashing the cash after the 1989 playoffs and offered me £30,000 for the season plus a massive Toyota Supra on three-year deal. But I didn't take it – in fact, I'm amazed I didn't take it!

After my trip to Edmonton the players treated me slightly differently. In the league the imported and top players were junior B and University guys from Canada, and they respected me for what I had done. It was something that some of the best players in our league hadn't achieved. There was nobody at the level I had been at in Canada. Of course, that meant it got a little tougher. They would smash me around a bit and I got some real heavy checks.

I did get a lot of questions about why I returned when the Oilers offered me the chance to stay. The fact is that people go to these things in America and come back all the time. Maybe they weren't offered enough money. Maybe they aren't good enough. Maybe the organisation wants them to try again a year later. It happens all the time. In my case, you had to look at the team the Oilers had. There was no way I was going to make the side that year, so I was realistic and they were realistic. They tried to send me to the juniors and I didn't want to do that. I simply made the decision there and then that I wanted to come home and that was that. That was it – it was my own personal decision. Nothing put me off. I was answerable to nobody. Sather's offer gave me a real buzz, but it was one of those things I decided at the time, and that was it.

Although they had given me the chance to go back after the season, I didn't know whether they would follow it though. People say things, but things change. So throughout that season it didn't really play on my mind. I wanted to do well and keep in shape, but I also wanted Murrayfield to do well and for me to repay the faith they had shown in me.

It was an interesting year in Edinburgh. We won the Heineken League, Premier Division title for the first time by seven points from Dundee. We also picked up the Regal Scottish Cup, beating Ayr 9-4 in the semi and Dundee 7-6 in the final. We added the Scottish League title to this and Stevie Coombe and I also played in Denmark for the Great Britain Juniors (Under-21s) in Pool C at the World Championships under Alex Dampier, taking the bronze medal.

On the flipside, our player/coach Ian Ramsey left the club early doors to go to Bournemouth and Canadian Mike Jeffrey, who we signed from Fife as top scorer, fell downstairs and broke his ankle and had to go home. This was only thirty-one days before the transfer deadline so we signed Brian Burley. But Fife and the Canadian Association weren't happy with Brian's registration so we lost him for two weeks and had to play with just two imports. Winning the league that year was immense. Derek Reilly stepped up to be coach and Kelland, Fera and I really clicked.

But Wembley proved once again to be an unhappy hunting ground for us. In the playoff semi-final I picked up four assists in our 9-6 win over a very strong Dundee Rockets team, who we seemed to have one sign over that year. We didn't back it up in the final. In fact, it was a nightmare. My partnership with Rick Fera never performed and we were 6-1 down after two periods against Durham. In the first forty minutes we only managed 14 shots and this gave us too much to do. My brother Paul, who had returned from Solihull, collapsed with cramp in the last twenty and it became more difficult from there. Wasps' Mario Belanger was immense that day, with a hat-trick.

Back then, high-scoring matches were the norm. Attacking players didn't give two hoots about the defence, and although we relied on them, we didn't try to get back to help them out. Yes, it was a little unfair on Moray Hanson, but that's how hockey was played back then. Moray was one of the best netminders around then and he was conceding six a game! We all wanted to score that year and I finished with figures of 105 goals, 111 assists for 216 points, 28 points from 6 games in the playoffs and 56 points from 10 games in the Scottish Cup. I also scored my 300th goal against the Panthers in February, but my plus/minus must have been around minus 100! It's amazing how the game has changed so much.

I was completely shattered by the end of the season. With everything that had happened I suppose I ran out of steam and didn't perform in the playoffs. Back then we played two lines and sometimes with only eight players. We just faded towards the end of the season and Durham got off to a flyer and we never got back. Interesting fact: Derek's brother Glen Reilly refereed the final! Make of that what you will. One thing is for sure though: it certainly didn't help.

When the season had finished, I still had no idea if I would be heading to Edmonton again but, soon enough, I got a call asking me to travel over. Although Glen had said that returning back to Edinburgh would not affect my development in any way, they were very keen to see if I had improved at all. I was physically fitter and had put on a lot of muscle, but I didn't know if my game had improved. To be honest, I was surprised they had asked me back, but at least I knew what the camp was all about this time. Again, I first trained in Victoria and it paid off as I survived the camp until the end and did really well.

Accompanying me to the Cougars was Young Player of the Year Martin McKay, who had won the same Calgary training camp prize as I had. It was good to fly over with somebody and have a friend in

Victoria – but his driving skills left a lot to be desired. During our time there we were given a knackered old Ford Escort to drive, but I'm convinced there was something wrong with that thing. We had to push it everywhere because it wouldn't start, although I'm sure Martin had done something to it. It certainly kept us in shape. We also managed to drive into a 'drive thru' the wrong way, but I'm blaming Martin for that too!

This time, I even got a game for the Oilers. We played an exhibition against Team Canada and I got an assist on a Kevin Lowe goal. Team Canada were packed full of stars and that was a real highlight of my career – actually pulling on the Oilers shirt.

At the end of the camp I was called into Glen's office and he asked me to stay. The Oilers wanted me to play in Nova Scotia but I again said no. I obviously wanted to play in the NHL and perhaps I was a little naive. Being over there would have been quite intimidating for me and I couldn't see the progression through the NHL. Some of the guys who played in Nova Scotia had been around for many years and they hadn't moved. Also, the money was horrendous. They offered me CD$25,000, which meant I would have actually have made more in Edinburgh! I had to be realistic – that amount of money would have left me struggling. They would have trained and played me, but I just felt it wasn't right.

Looking back, I should have probably have given it a year or two over there, but I made the decision at the time and I stuck with it. It just didn't feel right. There's no other explanation for it. People may think there was something that popped out and something happened, but it just didn't feel right for me. No one said I wouldn't make it. Regrets? Obviously, I have a few. Could I have made it? Glen Sather seemed to think so. It's not something I am worried about. If you sit and think about things in the past, they will tarnish your future.

Glen was disappointed I had not taken the deal. He said I had great ability and was a real prospect. I recently found out that he was surprised that I had not taken it. He said I really would have stood out in the NHL and my progress would have been celebrated. He was a real knowledgeable guy so it was nice for him to say that. Looking back, I wish he had said that at the time – certainly I would have tried to re-negotiate his appalling offer!

I have great respect for Glen in the way he treated me and he understood why I couldn't stay. Once he came into the dressing room after we played Canada in Pool A in Italy and asked to speak to me. He was and still is world famous, and the dressing room was buzzing. It was a real classy thing for him to do. We'd just got beat so I asked him if they took it easy on us, and he said yes. Canada could have killed us that year!

Hindsight is a wonderful thing and perhaps I should have stayed over there, but it was a great experience for me personally and it put British hockey on the map.

These days I'm surprised there haven't been more draft picks from the UK. Just look at some of the British players that could and should have been drafted. Jonathan Weaver got close, ending up in the East Coast League with Mississippi Sea Wolves and turning out for the Detroit Vipers in the International League before injury blighted his career. One player who could have gone all the way was David Longstaff. Perhaps as a player he matured too late but he certainly would have made it. He had as much ability as anyone and was big and strong with loads of pace – a fantastic player. If he had been born in Canada, he would have been in the NHL. He would have been better prepared than I was. If anyone had the ability, it was him and I truly believe he would have had a long career over there. Perhaps he stayed too long in Newcastle (being a homebird like me) and that didn't interest the scouts. He did play in Sweden for Djurgardens IF Stockholm, but that probably came too late for him to be drafted.

Colin Shields became the second player to be drafted from these shores in 1999 and is currently back in the UK at the Belfast Giants. He was selected by Philadelphia in the sixth round (195th overall) at the age of twenty after playing a handful of games for the Paisley Pirates when aged fifteen, and moved to the States to give it his all. It was fantastic achievement for him and Britain but, with no disrespect to Colin, the move was really hyped up because he had come from nowhere and people automatically said he would make the NHL. This was a really big statement to make and put a lot of pressure on him. Colin skates well, has the talent and has a great shot, but to make the NHL, guys similar to my own size, like Colin, have to be unique unless they are really talented. Because of this it was always a tough job for him to do it. He plays well at GB level, but there is a big step between GB and the best level in the world. I think the fact he has been drafted is great, but you have to be realistic. He was bounced around the ECHL, playing for San Diego, Atlantic City and the Greenville Grrrowl and this suggests that making the NHL might be a step too far now. That's no disrespect to Colin; he's done really well, but that's the way it is over there.

All this may sound a bit negative but I would be more than happy if he gets there, as it is very hard to make the grade. Using Colin and I as an example, there are thousands of guys like us trying to make it over there. The fact he got drafted is amazing, but the chances he actually makes the cut are pretty remote. The recent player strike hasn't helped him either, because a new batch of youngsters have come through ready to battle for places.

In my view, the route that Colin took is the only way that British players will be selected now. He went away to the States at fifteen to live and breathe the sport. It would be great to get someone from Great Britain playing in the NHL but sadly we are not set up for it. Okay, there may be somebody who comes through and flies against the grain on this, but with the current set-up in the UK it is near impossible.

In terms of what they can play with, the coaching system is not good enough. I'm not saying that the system is rubbish; rather that those coaches have nothing work with. To make the NHL you need to be coached at the highest level, on the ice every day and with the top players in the world. You're not lucky to get to that level; it takes talent and hard work and dedication. Colin did everything to make it and sacrificed a lot to get there but you have to do that in North America. Perhaps the next drafted British kid will need to live over there from the age of ten. Britain is an average Pool B country now – the NHL teams look at top Pool A players in countries such as Slovakia, Sweden and Germany. They do not come here anymore.

Some people may see that as a sad situation to be in, but I don't suppose it is. If you are drafted you should be pleased, because hockey isn't a big sport in the scheme of things in the UK. It is a tough sport to come to the top in. There are hardly any facilities; we're not in the Olympics and we're not picking up lottery funding. There's nothing to bring the guys through. Those who make the NHL come from the top leagues in the world, where they train and play full-time. Everything is right for them.

Have we missed a trick here? I think so. Players throughout the 1990s and up to the present time have come in and taken the money, although you can't blame them for that, and that cash has gone out of the sport. I have been saying this for more than a decade. I think we have missed the boat. The top league has begun to develop youth players but it will take time and effort from everyone concerned.

The players will get through eventually, but they will have to beat out guys that have been professional and in that position for more than seven years. It's going to be hard before another Colin, Tony or David Longstaff comes through.

7

'WE USED TO LIGHT A FIRE TO KEEP WARM...'

There's an old cliché that says when something happens you draw a line in the sand and move on. That's exactly what I wanted to do when I got back from the camp. There was plenty of talk about what had happened over there, but I wanted to put that aside and get on with hockey. Thankfully, Murrayfield had been handed the task of competing in the European Cup after topping the Heineken League the year before, very early in the season.

I was worried that I would miss the games because I was over in Canada but fate meant I could ice for the Racers in our first continental adventure. Because only sixteen teams could play in the tournament and seventeen applied, the bright sparks at the IIHF thought it would be good idea for us to face Slavia Sofia, a Bulgarian side known for its players' tempers. In the first leg over there we gained an 8-5 win, where I grabbed 3+1, and in the second we trashed them 11-3 (I took 5+3). The home match was very tasty indeed. Slavia were probably the worst club any British side had faced in the cup and they decided to 'goon' it up at Murrayfield to see if they could rattle us. Both Chris Kelland and Paul Pentland were given their marching orders for fighting and as a result were expected to miss the semi-finals. However, this was overturned.

A month later, in November 1987, we travelled over to Rotterdam expecting to get a good thrashing and this we certainly did. We did not know what to expect and although scouting reports said we should beat our first opponents, Turbana Pandas of Rotterdam, our confidence lasted one period as we were swamped 17-2. Worse was to come as we got thumped 8-3 by Swedish champions IF Björklöven and then 24-0 by Cologne Sharks of Germany. It really was a case of amateurs versus pros. Those teams were crammed with at least fifteen experienced top NHL players – especially the Sharks. In that game we actually scored, but the official disallowed it, so we stuck it to him and complained – he looked at us as if to say, 'What's the point?'

To be fair, despite the professionalism of the teams, deep down we knew what we would get. We were semi-pro and it was a great experience and, dare I say it, a good holiday for the lads. We went over with big hopes but after the second period of the first game we looked at ourselves in the dressing room, baffled, and knew what we were in for. But that's part and parcel of the game. We thought we had a chance in Rotterdam, but that's life.

The guys got into some scrapes on that trip. We spent most of our off ice time drinking as well as winding each other up by leaving buckets of water over doors, rearranging hotel rooms, banging on doors and ordering loads of room service for each other. It was real fun and it was fair to say that hockey wasn't key on that trip.

And the players on the other teams could see the stark difference in the European leagues. You could tell that they were laughing at us, but who wouldn't with twenty-odd rampaging Scots to contend with? Before the final game, Cologne's players wore suits and we donned trackies and jeans – they thought it was hilarious. We came back from Europe with a feeling of collectiveness but also in no doubts at the difference of the calibre of leagues over there. Yes, Heineken had put £1.5 million into the league over three years, but that was paltry compared to the expense of the Swedish and German leagues.

In the meantime, Durham Wasps were beginning to prove to everyone that they would again be a force to be reckoned with. Up until December they had only two imports, relying on Brits for their success. They then signed a centreman from Elliot Lake in Ontario who would eventually prove to be one of the greatest imports to play the game in Britain. Step forward Rick Brebant. Rick was probably, apart from Chris Kelland and Alex Dampier, the first truly talented import. His arrival started an influx of really good players but he lasted the course. Rick was only supposed to be here a year, but ended up staying until 2004! He finished with 2,407 points as well as GB honours. He also proved to be a thorn in the Racers' side on many occasions.

Before he joined the Wasps they once again proved to be our nemesis. With Murrayfield sat on top of the league, we headed into our Norwich Union Cup final game in December full of confidence. I opened the scoring after just five seconds and it was nip and tuck all the way through a 4-4 opening period. Then we just fell apart and lost 11-5. At this time they had a great way of unsettling their opposition – their rink! Durham was certainly the worst venue I have ever played in. It only had one shower, no toilets and we had to light a fire in an old bucket to keep warm. It was worse when it rained – you'd get showered with drizzle flying through the broken windows. Health and Safety would have had a riot back then and I suppose you would get hanged for less these days. Durham's fans certainly made up for it though. They would get 3,000 a game and although the rink was diabolical the atmosphere was superb. They had no nets down the boards so players would hit fans all the time with the puck and wayward sticks – and they kept coming. We would injure a few, unintentionally, and there would be a fresh batch next game. I'm old fashioned and I do think, especially where I grew up, where the arenas weren't so nice and the equipment was bad, that a lot of players these days certainly take a lot for granted.

That loss against Durham threw us a little. We had been top of the league so we expected to win, but didn't. Personally I was disappointed but glad to be in Edinburgh. I still had no regrets about leaving Canada but was enjoying the surroundings and looking forward to the rest of the season. Murrayfield had recruited well and, although no players really stood out, I made a good connection with Mike Snell and Mike Holmes on the top line. In 36 league games I scored 81 goals, 111 assists for 192 points. That is an average of more than five a game. Nowadays, if you average something like 1.3, you are happy, but that's the way the league was back then. My 400th league goal came on 13 March with four goals against Whitley.

Looking at that roster, Scott Neil got 128 and defenceman Kelland got 93! It really was a poor league defensively – backed up by the fact that Mike Kelly got 81 points and he never scored as many during the rest of his career. The league was good to watch and the fans loved it. Although the level wasn't as good as it is now, there were more people coming to watch. It was really fun to play in those games back then and it was great to score and play decent hockey. You used to practise a couple of times a week, then get on the bus and you never had a pre-match meal – unless it was fish and chips.

Some players also used to drink before the games and some didn't turn up if they had had a bad night. Nowadays you'd get the sack. Once or twice I had a few before the game in my younger days, especially at a double-header weekend, but some players would have five or six in the morning! That would knock me out these days. Some got hammered and played and no one cared. Fitness levels were also horrendous. Chris Kelland was the first guy to lift weights and work on his fitness. Players never went to the gym and only scrimmaged as practice. I was lean and quick but I only really took it seriously, in terms of being super fit, by the early nineties.

I still ask myself if it was still a challenge after nearly eight years of playing in the league. Perhaps it wasn't too much of a challenge in terms of points grabbing, but as Murrayfield weren't winning every game, it still had that element of the unknown. That was the real challenge for me back then. Looking back, to be good at sports you have to be self-centred. I put the team first but of course I have my faults but I still think you need to have that level of arrogance and swagger or you won't get there.

Back then, I was the centre of attention and people wanted me to do something good and looked at me when I did something bad. I had to take the rough with the smooth. But all eyes were on me, which brought some great pressure. Thankfully, I have been fortunate enough to do well with all of the teams I have played with. I have had good and bad times but I have never been a person who has bragged. I always think if you treat people well, you will get that back – and that's how I have got on with life. I have not upset that many people, or stabbed them in the back. I could have come back from Canada and swaggered about the place, but I'm not like that. There are players at the bottom of the ladder who act like that but there are also a lot of good players and some who think they are better than they are. Winning makes it easier, losing means I like to keep my head down. Keeping a level head is key for me as there's always someone around to kick you up the butt if you're doing badly.

I certainly had a severe kick at the playoffs. We had finished top of the Heineken League and secured the Scottish League and Cup double but had a match-up with Durham in the semi-finals at Wembley. What happened can only go down as one of the most amazing things in the sport. I scored seven – a championship record – and Rick Brebant bagged six. Unbelievably they won 11-8! That still bites me to that day and will never happen again. The game was a real corker. Rick had scored a hat-trick within fifteen minutes and it was 7-7 after two periods. But we just couldn't close it out. Durham went on to beat favourites Fife in the final. It was another bitter disappointment. It was the second year we had lost in a final.

In the close season I got the opportunity to train with Genève-Servette from Geneva who were looking for an additional import. They started training in August so I decided it would keep me busy over the summer and could lead to something – plus, they offered me an amazing £1,000 a week for the privilege so I would have been daft to refuse it. And they put me up in an apartment too.

Flying out of London after a night at Paul Heavey's house in Peterborough, I had no idea what to expect. The training was pretty intensive and got me in good shape. After four weeks they asked me to stay and play with them in the top Swiss league. However, I would have been the fourth import, which would have meant sitting in the stands waiting for one of the other imports to get injured. Yes, the money would have been excellent, but I just wasn't prepared to do that. If I was good enough to make the team I wanted to play. Thanks but no thanks.

It was pretty weird over there. I used to get up in the morning, go to the rink and then go home. I knew no one so it was hard and they all spoke French. I did have a phrase book but it turns out that Scottish to French doesn't go very well! So I was back at Murrayfield for the 1988/89 season.

For some reason we didn't recruit very well that year. Don't get me wrong, we had a good squad, but with just seventeen players we were always going to struggle if we picked up injuries. We brought in Frenchmen Denis Paul and Louis Haman, who doubled up as coach, but he couldn't speak English and the team didn't gel. We got through that season on talent alone, certainly not coaching. Denis got injured after just three games and was replaced with Luc Beausoleil, who did great. But Kelland had some issues with his passport and that upset the defence somewhat early doors. Yet we started the season with a bang, winning 14 on the trot, but got hammered by Tayside at home 11-5 in the Norwich Union Cup and it went downhill from there.

Our European adventure also ended before it had begun. This time we faced Budapest's Ujpesti Dozsa at Murrayfield but lost 8-6. Then, on October 8, I grabbed a hat-trick and three assists as we tried to do whatever we could to overturn their one-goal advantage. But we finished just short, winning 9-8. It was a strange away trip for us. After the game, Stevie Coombe, Chris Kelland and Scot Neil arrived back in my hotel room with sore faces. They had been at the local pub and it looked like they had been hammered in more ways than one at some point during the night. It turned out that they had picked a fight with someone who had a broken leg, but who was also a boxer! Apparently, he one-punched all three! At least they saw the funny side, because we all stuck it to them. Next morning at breakfast they were all crowing about being beaten up by a one-legged man!

That was probably the highlight of the season! We finished runners-up in the Heineken League and won the Capital Foods Scottish League and Cup. I finished with figures of 86 goals with 126 assists for 212 points – my second best return – and secured my 1,000th point in just seven years. It's something I was immensely proud of, and still am. My 500th league goal came against the Panthers on 4 November.

Talking of milestones, I made my full debut in March 1989 for the GB senior team during the World Championships in Pool D. Arriving in Belgium, coach Terry Matthews had big hopes that we could be promoted – but we fell just short. We got off to a flyer, beating New Zealand 26-0 and then drawing with Romania 6-6. Our sole loss came against the hosts, 6-5, and that proved to be the turning point. An 8-4 win against Spain was scant consolation.

There were plenty of rumours when we returned about why it had not gone so well. It's true that I had a back problem, but I had always suffered from this from an early age. I was seeing a specialist on and off and we didn't know whether it was a kidney issue or something else. It meant that it was tough to fight players off but over time, through stretching and training, it cleared up. These days the advice for injuries is far better. You have to look at your 'core'. If you want a strong back it is important to work on your stomach too so it balances out and can 'carry' the rest of your body.

There was also talk that I turned up with no helmet and blunt skates, but I actually forgot my passport! I travelled with my coat and bag, but the rest of my kit went over with the trainers to save haulage money on the flight. I arrived at the airport ready, but my passport was on its way to Belgium! Yes, it was really embarrassing, but these days I always seem to forget something.

After the event, the Belgian authorities announced three players had been dope tested and that all were guilty of taking steroids. Their tests showed exactly the same result, and when I say the same result, I mean *exactly* the same result, which would be unusual with three people's tests. But the thing was, the cleanest guy you could ever think of, GB captain Gordon Latto, was named as one of the three. Because of that we had to forfeit our 26-0 win and Belgium finished top of the pool.

Playing for GB at any level was a real honour, but I do believe the authorities lost control of it for a while. Yes, it was good to go away, but I never received one penny for playing for GB. Don't get me wrong, I didn't want to be paid, but some players were getting paid for turning out – especially in the early 1990s. In the time of dual nationals I knew that most of the Canadian players got paid and that they asked for it. I know it was also kept quiet so other players, as well as the fans, didn't find out. I played with GB until 1994 and then I stopped for five years so some younger guys could get a chance. There was no real reason why I stopped, I was happy to play for the team and it was fun, but the money thing was annoying as it was unfair on everyone. I fully believe that some of the dual national players would not have played for GB if they hadn't got paid. That's my view anyway. I didn't think that was right. You should represent your country because you want to, not because you are being bunged a few bob.

In my view, the dual nationals boosted the quality of the team but at what cost? It was true to say that Ice Hockey UK wanted to get into Pool A so they thought it would be a good idea to bring these guys in and therefore get funding from the lottery and government. But when we got there, we simply weren't good enough to compete with the likes of Canada. We weren't strong enough.

Other teams' national programmes were far better and by saturating the GB team with dual nationals, it stopped quite a few youngsters being picked. Some of the dual nationals gave 110 per cent – the likes of Rick Brebant and Doug McEwen – it really brought them on as players, but there were too many in the national team. How can it be a national team with fourteen Canadians on a GB passport? We did need to add those players to the team, but not as many as that. We relied on them too much and it came back to bite us.

Nowadays we are looking to youngsters again and that has to be the way to go, but for a long time our national programme was non-existent and it will take time to come back.

8

'I STILL CANNOT WATCH
THAT GAME...'

Sometimes matches live in the memory for all the right reasons. I've been very lucky to taste several of these throughout my career so I don't let the negative games get to me. But sometimes the pressure of an event is too much. In 1990, we had reached our fifth Wembley playoff final in seven years and we were facing big-spending Cardiff, who had some great names on their roster including Steve Moria, Doug McEwen, Ian Cooper and Shannon Hope.

It was a real scary game to play in and really tight. We were 3-0 up within about sixteen minutes with two through Mollard either side of a Scott Neil goal. I picked up two assists on the first two goals, although on the first one I actually fell over but managed to poke check the puck before I hit the deck. But for some reason we took our foot off the gas when we looked to be in complete control. First Moria caught us two on one and passed to Ian Cooper, who slotted home, then he got one off to McEwen who one-timed it to make it 3-2. Within seconds there was a scramble at the net and Moria found the top corner. Three-all after looking so comfortable.

The second period was really cagey until I managed to slip McKee a great pass to make it 4-3. That was how it ended, and the third period was real end-to-end stuff. We scored an early marker through Neil to make it 5-3 before Ian Cooper pulled one back. I then slotted home to take us two clear before McEwen scored a blinder – one of those where it really looked like the puck was glued to his stick as he danced through the defence.

Then a piece of plexi-glass broke, which took fifteen minutes to fix, and both teams, refreshed, went for it again. We did sit back a little before the end of the period and Stephen Cooper made it 6-6 with just ninety-five seconds to go. It was gutting. To be up all the way and for them to come back was a blow. But we felt strong going into the first sudden-death overtime period in the championship's history. It was great for the capacity 9,000 crowd who lapped it up, but even that couldn't separate us, despite both teams having chances, and it went to penalty shots.

Penalty shots are a very unfair way of finishing a game, but great drama for the fans. Leo Koopmans, our coach, picked five guys and we were straight into sudden death. The idea is to skate from centre ice and beat the keeper. Very simple... sort of. Before you take one, you need a plan. The thing you must do is hit the net and at least make the keeper work for it. You also have to decide whether to go at the netminder slow or fast. To be honest, it can be a lottery. For some reason, the five guys continue to take shots even if they have missed one. The ice at Wembley was atrocious that year and became really bumpy towards the end of overtime. It meant that the puck bobbled all over the place and it was a lot harder to get a sweet hit on it. I don't know what happened, and looking back all the shots are a blur, but Jeff Smith saved all three of my penalties to hand the cup to the Devils. Time after time I have played that game over in my head and perhaps nerves got the better of me. Lining up for the first shot I was incredibly nervous and my mind went blank. It was a tame effort. The other two I simply cannot remember, although I am reminded by various sets of supporters on a constant basis. I know I needed to score on the last shot to even it up, but Jeff saved it and I smashed my stick against the goal in frustration. Cardiff's players went bananas.

For the record, in the first round Lawless, McEwen and Moria scored for Cardiff with Mollard, Kelland and McKee making it 3-3.

In the second, Lawless and Moira scored again with Neil and Mollard evening it up for the Racers. In the third, McEwen gave Cardiff the lead and the rest is history.

After the game I was inconsolable and cried my eyes out in the dressing room. It was my responsibility to bring the cup home and I failed to do it. The guys were so deflated and I was upset for them. It meant everything to us; we had gone so far as the underdogs and I felt I had let my teammates down. All these years later it is still tough to think about that game. I have never watched it, such is the hurt I feel. And I never will. But you have to move on. A few years later I was involved in another shootout with Sheffield and I was the fifth guy. It was playing on my mind but thankfully our netminder Wayne Cowley saved it and I didn't need to take one. I would have no problem taking one now, because I have the experience, but back then I was young and the nerves got to me. Now, I have two moves to use when I come down the ice and I would stick to them.

It had been a half-decent season up until then. Although we finished runners-up in the Heineken League, we took the Scottish Cup and League double and avenged a few demons by beating the Wasps at the Playground in Basingstoke 10-4 to take the Norwich Union Cup. The highlight of that game was undoubtedly the first bout of fisticuffs on national television, when Kelland and Brebant just went for it in a big way. It was a real cracker of a scrap with neither giving anything away. Rick is a tough little bugger though and he just shaded it. The media devoted columns and columns to it afterwards and discussed in great detail how the game had been lifted or degraded.

I think you have to have some fights in a game to keep the interest up. If you talk to someone who doesn't watch the sport they will always ask about the fights before the score. But, you have to know when to do it. I've coached and played with some tough guys who are ready for a ruck all the time. If the fight is done at the right time and the person wins, it can make a serious difference to the team and be the difference between winning and losing.

I didn't and don't fight that that much, but the one that sticks out is the one with Gareth Owen in Coventry when I was the player/coach for Dundee Stars. He nipped the puck off me and he seemed to catch my knee with his stick, which span me around. As the play progressed and I picked myself off the ice, the Blaze nearly scored so as he came back I had a word in his ear. But for some reason he kept staring at me, and I didn't know whether he wanted to go for it or not so I hit him once. But there was not much in it to be honest.

Another highlight was winning MVP for GB in March 1990. Our Pool D matches in Cardiff were a real walkover as we beat Australia 14-0 and 13-3 and Spain 13-1 and 17-3. That was really embarrassing. In the future we would get some thrashings ourselves but we gave those teams a good tonking. It was so one-sided we could have beaten them in our sleep. To be honest we wanted the Aussies to get something out of the games, as they were great guys. They had come over for a laugh and were great people to get along with. Our objective was just to get promoted and it wasn't much of a challenge.

9

'THEY THREW NEEDLES AT ME WHEN I WASN'T PLAYING...'

A poor campaign the previous year had rattled us and we wanted to make amends going into 1990/91. But this season, especially the climax, would always hold some of the most painful memories the sport has given me. We had recruited well that year and the top line of myself, Jock Hay and Scott Neil really clicked. We had replaced Brian McKee, who incidentally had the hardest shot I have ever seen – he injured keepers with it – with some quality, and we all seemed to gel as a team. In 34 games I scored 60 goals, with 96 assists for 156 points and Jim Mollard had a great season with 108 points. We won the Capital Foods Scottish Cup once again, my 600th league goal came against Durham on 23 February and I set up a Norwich Union Cup record with 11 assists against Trafford Metros in the quarter-final.

I also played in Pool C with Britain, but we failed to get promoted, finishing a disappointing fifth, with hosts Denmark taking the medal. We also lost to those Wasps again, 11-6 in the semi-final of the Heineken Championships at Wembley, despite leading 6-4 after the second. They also beat us 12-6 in the Norwich Union Cup.

After the end of the season I was appointed by the BIHA to be British ice hockey's representative on the British Olympic Competitors' Council, which was a great honour. I was also on the

Players' Association to meet with the league. At that time, and indeed this holds true today, it was important for the players to have a voice. Some leagues in the past have not been interested in the players. For instance, the Elite League have made some decisions that are good for the players, but also some that are bad as well, and they are not interested, in my view, in what we think. We currently play with ten imports – would it make any difference if we cut it to nine? Wouldn't it be good PR? Would it save money? Wouldn't it be good for the British game?

Hockey was undergoing some major changes back then with sponsorship and the amount of money heading into the game was beginning to get scary. At the time I didn't know what was happening with the sport so I have to admit I was looking around to check my options. The *Sunday Express* quoted me as saying: 'I reckon I will play for another three or four years, but if a really good job came along, who knows?' Later in the season, *The Guardian* reported I had joined the police. Of course, it wasn't true but it was on my mind. I didn't know how long hockey would last for me, but I loved playing and it was in my blood. As I pondered my options, I was hit with an eight-game ban for a drug offence.

To say I was gobsmacked would be an understatement. The ban would mean I would miss the first month of the 1991/92 season. I had been tested at Peterborough and they had found traces of ephedrine in my system. At the time I had told the tester that I had taken a decongestant tablet to clear up a bad cold and they had said it was fine. But back then, apart from the odd card with details on what we had to look out for, we were given no advice on what we could or could not take. When it came back positive I asked them to test the 'B' sample straightaway, just in case they had made a mistake, although it was very seldom wrong. Most athletes know now that if you are caught from the 'A' sample, the 'B' is going to back it up. Perhaps I asked them to check because I was so flabbergasted.

I'm not sure if ephedrine is still banned but it is supposed to pump you up if you take it in the right doses. It provides the kick that energy drinks can give you and the amount in my system was equivalent to drinking two litres of Coke. Ridiculous.

At my hearing with the league in London the punishment that was handed down was nothing short of completely scandalous. The last person who had been collared got two games and I believe to this day that because it was me and the success I had enjoyed, they wanted to make an example. It was reduced to six games on appeal, but I believe that any player other than Tony Hand would have got a lesser sentence.

Actually, players did get caught in the years to come for the same offence and got a lesser ban. Of course, they were right, it was in my system, but it wasn't through any foul means or anything like that to improve my game. Now, if I was unsure, I wouldn't take it.

What happened afterwards has played on my mind ever since. I got letters sent to the rink with needles in them and others calling me a druggie. It was awful. The press wrote that this was the worst thing to happen to British Ice Hockey and when I was playing, crowds would chant 'druggie' at me. And at Fife they threw syringes down at me when I wasn't playing. It truly was a horrendous time. It was terrifying in fact. I felt like a drug addict. People made up what they thought it was and didn't or wouldn't listen to the facts. Someone came straight up to my face and called me, and I quote, a 'junkie bastard'. People seem to forget that I was only twenty-three at the time.

By the time my ban had finished and I started playing it had knocked my confidence quite a bit. People did think I was taking steroids and all sorts of stuff, because I had done well and people thought it was the drugs. I certainly kept a low profile for a while after that.

After missing those penalty shots and now this, it was the lowest point of my career.

10

'I THOUGHT ABOUT TRYING
THE POLICE FORCE...'

Murrayfield was always one of those clubs that was there or thereabouts at the end-of-season shake-up, but it was getting harder and harder to compete in a burgeoning league. Sponsorships were coming thick and fast, teams were throwing around some big money and the traditional heartlands of Scotland – Dundee, Fife and ourselves – began to have difficulty attracting talent from the likes of Cardiff and Nottingham who were offering bigger salaries. As a result, the league was flooded with imports and this no longer included junior B and University players. Clubs had NHL guys on their rosters. Because these players were signing for southern clubs, Scottish hockey really struggled to attract the best the game could offer. In Edinburgh, our team was getting older despite youngsters coming through, so like the rest we had to look to imports to bolster the squad in a market we couldn't really compete in.

Our roster in the 1991/92 season was massive because we had a ridiculously high turnover of imports. Thankfully, Leo Koopmans came back as coach to give the team some stability, we retained a strong 'spine' of myself, Paul Hand and Scott Neil and Hanson and Martin McKay shared the netminding duties, but no fewer than three players played one game and left.

We recruited Dave Shyiak from the Northern Michigan University who did really well, getting 54 points in just 27 games before he got injured and left. Ian Pound (#221 overall 1985 NHL Draft) went the same way, as did Jason Hannigan. We never seemed to get the right blend in the side, although Kyle McDonough came in and did well with 93 points in just 28 games. Kyle was a real livewire, recruited from the East Coast Hockey League's Raleigh Icecaps, and was apparently good friends with *Happy Gilmore* actor Adam Sandler.

The club also seemed to be at loggerheads with the BIHA all season. In October we were fined £50 for icing Canadian junior B player Roger Hunt when he wasn't properly registered, and then a further £500 for ignoring written instructions not to ice the player. Leo was fined £100 for his comments on the affair. Roger would later make sure his appearance in British Ice Hockey would be memorable by flooring Bracknell's Lee Odelein during a stoppage in play, breaking his jaw and cheekbone and giving him a hefty concussion. Roger was banned for life because of this incident, as was Leo. It meant that Jock Hay stepped up to become coach.

Despite the fun and games with the roster I still continued to enjoy the game. Before the season started I was once again quoted in the papers expressing doubts on how the sport was shaping up in the UK. I said, 'I think the way the game is going, with the money and everything, is pretty scary. I hear stories of… guys you never hear of… getting half-decent money. They way it is going you cannot be sure hockey is going to be around in two or three years. I've actually been speaking to the police force and I've got my letter away to apply.'

Ice hockey had no big stadiums at the time and there was uncertainty. You also did not get paid during the off season. I had no family to support back then, but I had a mortgage, and I thought about trying the police force. But, after looking into it, the shifts would have affected when I could play so I would have had to give up my sport.

At the time Murrayfield certainly weren't big payers but I was personally sponsored by Capital Foods, which helped immensely. After a while this dried up as the firm faced stiff competition from bigger food providers and went into liquidation. Perhaps what had happened with the dope test had given me second thoughts on the sport. Who knows? Yet, when I started the season late after the six-game ban I got into my stride quickly and had a good year, although the team didn't.

Individually, I picked up a wealth of accolades, probably my most to date. I was named in the BIHWA All-Star team (Forward), was Players' Player of the Year, leading scorer and won the Pool C Best Forward award at the World Championships.

I also captained Scotland in the 49th Home International in December 1991. Playing for my country was a real honour and something I always enjoyed. Although the matches are never classics they do provide entertainment for the fans. I scored a hat-trick as we won 7-6. We were 4-0 up and then they tied it up before we got ahead once again.

In my view these games are vital for the sport. It was enjoyable and the players enjoyed it too, but it seems like the business side of the game is far too important. The difference between financial success and failure is a fine line these days. But hasn't the sport lost some of its identity because of this? If you are putting together a fixture like this, the teams will automatically ask if they will make any money out of it. You can see where they are coming from, as they would need to release players and probably lose a weekend's fixtures.

All I ask is what about the bigger picture? Don't they think the international team would benefit? I understand it is a business and we have to look at that. It would be a great draw but if a team loses a home fixture that makes a big dent in the profitability of an outfit.

After the success of the GB team the previous year, we needed to use that experience to compete well in Pool C at the World Championship, and we certainly did that, taking the gold medal to be promoted to Pool B. Held in March 1992 at the Humberside Ice Arena in Hull, we finished top of the group, ahead of North Korea, Australia, Hungary, Belgium and South Korea, not losing a game in the process. I had a flyer in the tournament – as did the team – and finished top scorer with 18 points from 5 games. We beat North

Korea 16-2 where I assisted a perfect shortie that probably turned the game. Up 1-0 at 9.41 with the Koreans on a 5 on 3, I won possession, killed off a few seconds and slipped in Stephen Cooper for a SH. At that point we knew the group was there for the taking.

I finished the season with 140 league points (60 goals, 80 assists), on a line that was never really settled. I played with Jock and Scott Neil up until December when Jock retired, then with Jason Hannigan and sometimes with Kyle. With everything that happened it was always going to be tough for the Racers to compete. The roster changes didn't help, and Leo's ban was a shocker, but the dressing room remained strong. We finished fifth in the league and won the Capital Foods Challenge Series but had a disaster in the Autumn Cup and didn't make Wembley. Something needed to change if we were ever going to compete again with the likes of Durham, Cardiff and Nottingham.

11

'ENTER THE NUTTER…'

There are some players that fans can instantly remember. Gretzky, Messier, Unger, Howe. They're all names that bring back fond memories, great goals, amazing plays and touches of genius. Ask a player who they remember as 'the best' and you'd probably get the same answer. Yet, sometimes names stick in the mind for a long time – and it's not just down to playing expertise.

If there's one thing that British ice hockey fans enjoy more than anything it's a good ruck, and in 1992, up at Murrayfield Ice Rink, they got the opportunity to see one game after game. Everyone at the club knew that the previous season had been a disaster on and off the ice so we looked to make amends. Early doors we recruited well with Ontario-born Chris Palmer and third-round draft pick John Newberry coming in to form a top line with me, and we clicked all year.

Palmer was a great goalscorer and John had played for the Montreal Canadiens. He was a big guy, not a great skater but had the best set of hands I have ever seen on a player. He knew how to play hockey and knew he had played the game at a higher level.

Coaches Derek Reilly and Jock Hay also bolstered our roster with a former Edmonton Oilers third-round draft pick to strengthen the defence. What happened next can only be described as mayhem! Enter the nutter, Mike Ware.

Mike was, and in my view still is, the toughest guy to play over here. He was 6ft 6ins, 215 pounds and no one had ever seen the likes of him before. I once asked the former GB coach Chris McSorley who was the toughest guy to play in the league and he named Mike straight away. He said Ware scared him the most as you had no idea what he was going to do. If something went in his head then he would do something really dumb like stick a guy or just go crazy.

Having played with Mike for years, Chris was certainly right. Mike was a classy player – he would score points from all over the place, but he was a complete nutter! It's fair to say that Mike was my protector along with my brother when he came to the club. I rarely got myself into trouble but Chris Palmer really got on opposing players' nerves and Mike would go right in there and get stuck in.

Over the years, his antics have been the stuff of legend. A real crazy moment was when he was playing in Germany for Hanover Scorpions. A guy high-sticked him and knocked two of his teeth out. As the player went off the ice to the penalty Mike went for him and claimed he had done it on purpose, which, apparently, he hadn't. Next time he played against him he didn't tell any of his teammates what he was going to do, but in the warm-up he went straight over to the guy, high-sticked him and then proceeded to give him an absolute hammering. He knew there would be no cameras during the warm-up so realised it was his chance! Feeling pretty pleased with himself back in the dressing room, there was a knock of the door. When it opened there was a load of police officers waiting for him – just like a scene from *SlapShot*. As he was led away Mike was trying to protest his innocence! It was really calculating and that's what was scary. He had thought about it, where the cameras would be and carried it out. He recently said to me that he never got him as good as he should have! Mike is one of my best mates despite his craziness.

That season the team's penalties certainly went up. I clocked 100 penalty minutes, more than ever before, and I lay the blame firmly at Mike's door. He used to kick it off and we all piled in. Although he calmed things down a lot, he never started anything unless he thought he was wronged. And this happened a lot. We would tell him in the dressing room afterwards that the other guy didn't touch him after he had given him a good pounding and Mike would say, 'Alright then, he nearly touched me!'

Mike's antics certainly gelled the team and we finished as Capital Foods Scottish Cup Winners and runners up behind Cardiff in the Heineken League – a far better return than the previous year. I scored 185 (66 goals, 119 assists) in the league and 33 points in our play-off run. My 700th league goal came against Durham in December 1992 in my 362nd game. Unfortunately, the team set another marker – being the only team to be nilled in the playoffs. It was supposed to be a classic in the making, but Cardiff stuck nine past us in the semi in a game I unsurprisingly don't like to think of that often. Two shifts into the game I took a heavy hit and thought I had torn my ligaments. It proved to be a bruised knee and I carried on with lots of ice in between plays.

During the season all eyes were on our World Championship Pool B matches in Holland as the press and the authorities believed we could make it to Pool A – and games against the likes of Canada and the Soviets. But beforehand, the fiftieth Home International at Sheffield proved that organisation was not the sport's greatest asset. It was a real mess. Although we (Scotland) won 5-4, and I scored two goals and an assist, England's players did not turn up with enough shirts to wear and had to don white tops. The competition was also unsponsored. I was quoted as saying, 'The game might have been a lot better if we could have got together beforehand.' This is certainly true. It was very amateurish. If it was built up, the players picked and scouted right then it would better. But the selection wasn't great to be honest. And the players, realising it was badly run and poorly organised, switched off. The following year nine players failed to show. In the end, the fans lost.

If the BIHA couldn't organise a Home International then questions needed to be asked regarding how, if we got into Pool A, we could compete with the likes of America. But we had to get there first. Heading over to Holland, all the players were confident of success and we had a right to be. We had been promoted twice on the run and the dual internationals such as Fera and Mason, whatever the moral reasons for using them, certainly bolstered the team. We also went through a heavy schedule of eight warm-up games throughout the season.

Perhaps we underestimated how well we could play because we murdered everyone, finishing top of the group without a loss. Great Britain beat China 14-0, Romania 10-4, Bulgaria 10-0, Denmark 4-1, Japan 5-4, Holland 3-2 and Poland 4-3. I scored 14 points in 7 games and the experience was great.

We certainly weren't ready for Pool A, but we were very grateful that we had the opportunity to compete with the best. But the following year we didn't do ourselves any favours. The main bulk of the GB team played at Wembley in the playoffs and then went straight into the games up against teams that had been together for three weeks or more.

It seemed that although Heineken was putting thousands of pounds into the sport, none was available for a really good and successful training camp. It left us badly prepared.

12

'THERE'S NO POINT IN HAMMERING THESE GUYS...'

So we made it. Pool A. The game's elite. This was the renaissance of British ice hockey and an opportunity to put the game on the lips of the nation's public. Played in Bolzano, Canazei and Milan in Italy between 25 April and 8 May 1994, it was our chance to test ourselves at the highest level and, if we retained our group status by avoiding relegation, an opportunity to give the game a much needed financial shot in the arm. Sad then, that the whole affair bordered on farce.

Straight after the playoffs we headed over to Italy to take part in the competition with no training camp or planning. We were unprepared to take on the best in the world and, my god, did it show. As a team we were pretty close-knit, and looking at our fixtures we expected a tough run but also thought that we could give a good account of ourselves.

In our first match against Russia we were crushed 12-3. We were six down after the first period and I remember looking round the dressing room and seeing how the other GB players felt – clearly like we were out of our depth. A day later we lost 4-0 to Germany, with inspired netminding from Martin McKay keeping the score down. Two days later Italy beat us 10-2, and then Canada took it easy on us, winning 8-2. One of their defencemen was actually quoted in the papers saying, 'There's no point in hammering these guys. So we just played river hockey.' Glen Sather also said the same when he came to visit me in our dressing room.

On 3 May Austria blanked us 10-0. We then had a relegation play-off against Norway and, despite it being 2-2 at the end of the second, lost 5-2.

Seeing those results now doesn't half bring back some bad memories. I was as guilty as most as I never performed and wasn't in the best shape anyway. But we simply weren't ready. After the last match Alex Dampier said that Great Britain was a Pool B nation, and how right he was.

Other teams went away for a month to prepare, we went straight after the playoffs and were just completely out of our depth. We weren't mentally ready to face these top internationals and physically we struggled. It was an incredible experience to test yourself against these players but actually playing in those hammerings was gut-wrenching.

Personally, it was a real low point. I thought I would be fine against these guys, but I just didn't perform. I, as well as the whole organisation, underestimated how good these teams were. We went as Pool B champions and thought we could make the step up, and we were confident, but it just wasn't enough. We shouldn't have been at that level – perhaps we were promoted a year or two early. We played at a Pool B level. Teams we should have beaten turned us over. We were a laughing stock and it showed that the level in this country was not good enough. It was a real wake-up call.

The dual-national issue was always a big thing for me. While they did improve the quality of the squad, some of their actions left a bitter taste. I know, as I have said before, that some got paid while the Brits didn't, but when we played Canada and I looked down our line and saw Rick Fera, hand on heart, belting out the Canadian anthem, I was upset. It's also fair to say that a lot of the GB team got pretty angry. I don't think I could play for America and sing the Scottish anthem – it wasn't the way it should be done.

When we played Norway for that final relegation game, before the match we were approached by our team bosses and offered money to stay in the Pool. To say I was shocked was an understatement. It came completely out of the blue and it seems when the BIHA realised relegation would hit its pockets, it tried to spur us on with money.

It was all a bit cheesy. Money was never an object with some of the players and now it mattered all of a sudden. It actually cost some players money to be there. That money should have gone into training camps – it should have been upfront at the beginning. Having guys pumped up for money isn't right. If you have to be offered money as an incentive – especially for your country – then what's the point?

As a coach I have offered players cash out of my own pocket. You know – the guy who scores the game winner gets £200, that sort of thing. But asking your national team to win and telling them they will then receive a bonus is just plain wrong. Looking back it really demotivated me.

We had also done poorly in the Olympic qualifiers towards the back end of 1993, with 3 losses and 1 draw. Perhaps this should have been a warning sign for Pool A in 1994? Even on home ice we could not beat teams that we probably should have. Slovakia won 7-1. We lost 8-4 to Latvia, Japan beat us 4-2 and we drew 2-2 against Poland. Alex changed the winning Pool B team and brought in another four imports and the team didn't gel.

That was it for me. After the Olympic qualifying, Pool A showing, poor organisation and the whole issue of money I decided not to play for GB again. It was a hard decision, but I wanted to give some of the younger guys the chance to compete. I didn't enjoy it and I didn't want to know about it unless it got run properly.

Nowadays we would be better prepared, but our national programme isn't up to it. These young British guys can handle the pressure and get back to Pool A. All it takes is the right training, organisation and, above all, motivation from the leagues and teams.

13

'I REMEMBER TURNING UP AT THE RINK AND "STEALING" OUR EQUIPMENT...'

Derek Reilly and his partner Robert Adams had bought the Murrayfield Racers at the beginning of the 1992/93 season and brought some much-needed stability to the team. They also managed to keep hold of Smirnoff, who had wanted to pull out, as sponsor.

We felt with some solid foundations that we could begin to compete with the 'bigger' teams, and had proved that the previous season. Going into 1993/94 the organisation wanted to put last season behind it and get back on an even keel. For me, I was just glad to be a part of a really good dressing room and was looking forward to Pool A. How wrong could I be? Pool A was a disaster and the year as a whole couldn't have got much worse.

It began brightly with Rocky Saganiuk being brought in as coach, Frank Morris and Richard Laplante following him and Moray Hanson returning from the old enemy Fife. We also signed British player Dean Edmiston. It was a very talented roster with Richard, Frank and Chris Palmer being standout players. Dean was a real ducker and diver. He always seemed to be up to something and my brother Paul was doing what he did best, fighting and scoring!

The team as a whole clicked once again and before 1994 we had wrapped up the Benson and Hedges Cup final against Cardiff with Hanson getting Man of the Match with a brilliant display between the pipes. It was our first major trophy in three years. I scored two goals in a 6-2 win against a superb team that contained Doug McEwen, Rick Brebant, Hilton Ruggles and John Lawless. It was a really good performance and Hanson just kept locking the door every time we scored, eventually turning away 39 shots.

We finished fourth in the league, but were deducted five points for breaking wage-capping regulations and didn't make Wembley. My 800th league goal came against Bracknell on 20 March 1994, a day when I came away with 3 goals and 8 assists and I finished with 222 points (72 goals, 150 assists) – something I was really pleased about until I read recently that Tricky (Rick Brebant) got 273!

We had the makings of a real championship-winning team but fate once again conspired against us. Halfway through the season the owners stopped paying the players and claimed that the lack of fans was the main root cause. Later in the season those same fans raised £30,000 to keep us afloat. It turned out that the relationship between the team and the rink had become strained due to unpaid bills. They shut us out of the facility in April and we had to play our final playoff group game around fifteen miles away in Livingston. We had already played one match in Kirkcaldy and only one at Murrayfield. I remember a load of us turning up at the rink and running out with our equipment because they weren't going to let us in to get it. It got really bad and I knew after that happened it was always going to be a downward spiral for the team. Although the team couldn't pay us, a guy called Kenny Mclen, who still sponsors the club, was giving us money out of his own pocket. There are some great guys in hockey and he never asked for anything in return.

Looking back, the rink probably wasn't at fault; they just wanted the money that was owed to them. After the playoffs, the team's owners went back to the rink to sort it out and it just didn't get going. In the end, Stuart Robertson bought the team and renamed it the Edinburgh Racers as Murrayfield Racers Ltd was expelled from the league owing money to the rink and the BIHA.

It was a really sad and frustrating time. When we weren't being paid, it made the players strong as a unit because we were all playing for each other. Having joined the Players' Association that year and being team captain I was negotiating on behalf of the team to ensure they got paid. Rocky was siding with the management, as would be expected, although I'm sure he was in a difficult position. But as soon as Rocky realised he wasn't getting paid either he wanted to join our side. As we were a strong bunch of guys I had to turn him down.

I wasn't envious of Rocky at all. He wanted to join us all along but was placed in an impossible situation. He would say, 'You play and we'll be okay' and things like that but in the end we weren't getting a bean for putting our bodies on the line. He couldn't give the team a hard time for not playing and then turn round and want to be a part of that team. There was never any talk of a player boycott though.

In the end it really affected us and the league position reflected that. Not only were we struggling financially, but we also had points deducted for a breach of the wage cap. These wage caps are a farce in my view. If you are going to do it properly, you should do it. They made an example of us but I have no doubt other teams did the same – we were the only team to get investigated.

The type of wage cap and how it should be introduced depends on what the league is all about. If you get a bunch of directors who agree to the cap and then do not follow it, then what's the point? Some teams will then follow it, thinking there is an agreement, while others will not. As a player I would rather not have a cap – but that's obvious! However, such a situation means that some coaches look great when they are coaching an expensively assembled team, when actually they're not, they have just spent more. If your team spends more then the law of averages says that you will do better.

In 2005 there was a very loose cap and some clubs pushed very hard to have one introduced. The basic cap is based around an agreement between the clubs. I know what players get offered and I know the market and I know the costs to bring them in, because they talk. They all know who is at it. Are a lot of teams sticking to it? I wouldn't like to comment, but if everyone looked in the mirror perhaps they couldn't answer such a question. Some clubs would deny it, but the players are on incentives to come over.

So how much does it cost to bring in a player? In 2005 you were looking at around £300 to £500 a week. That's not megabucks and it is nothing that the player is going to retire on. If you offer a guy £500 and another team offers £600, you know where that player is going to go. At one point it looked like wages were going to go through the roof but the gravy train is now gone.

Towards the end of the nineties Glen Anderson, an NHL player, wanted £7,000 a week to play for Cardiff. My good friend Mike Ware was at Cardiff at the time and said the whole affair was a circus. Glen would turn up in a limo to play the game and in my view he came across for the holiday. You have to ask if he was of sound mind. Who in their right mind comes over here, sees the type of rinks they are playing in and asks for seven grand a week? That's ridiculous. You just don't do that sort of thing. I would be surprised if Cardiff would have paid that but I'm sure they offered him a good package. But it was all about the money. Thank god they turned it down, but I'm sure they could have got close to affording it.

When a team puts together a roster they will look at getting the right blend for their budget. For example, Team A could have seven players at £500 whereas Team B could have three at the same amount and the rest at £300. The difference is that some teams get more quality out of their budgets. Some will pay £250 for their last guy when others can afford £450. Owners have to tread a fine line between what the fans want – success – and what they can afford to pay. It's a real game of cat and mouse.

When you look at it, an average salary of £2,000 a month for a top player is not a lot for the work he will put in. In my view sometimes the owners ask too much of their players and perhaps there should be a more enforceable minimum wage. Players these days have to be full-time professionals as they travel all over the place and get battered for seven to eight months. Nine out of ten players certainly earn their money. But it's a business for the player and the team. If a player can get £50 or £100 more elsewhere, he will.

Coaches' wages are slightly different – fifty per cent of their wages come under the salary cap. I once read something that suggested I was on a six-figure deal. Six figures? I would kill for that. The most I have ever been on was towards the back end of the decade when I was paid £950 plus bonuses at Sheffield. And that was great money. I was leading the league in scoring at that time and the club were attracting 10,000 spectators a game. It wasn't as if I wasn't paying my way!

But if there is to be a successful capping situation then it needs to be set in stone. What I'm saying is that if you go in at boardroom level and ten directors want a cap, but when you leave four continue to pay above that level, then how can you win? If you have a cap it has to be enforced. If you don't agree to it, don't vote for it. There needs to come stronger governance for the good of all.

14

'WE DIDN'T KNOW
HE HAD BEEN IN A MENTAL
HOSPITAL…'

With a new team name and new owners most of the players looked at the Edinburgh Racers at the back end of 1994, with a feeling of excitement. It was always going to be a big ask on and off the ice to rebuild again but thankfully the new ownership managed to keep hold of a good nucleus of the previous year's roster.

It meant that while it was effectively a new team, it had a familiar look to it. To be fair it was pretty sad when Murrayfield Racers Ltd had to liquidate. They had been a part of my life since I started skating at the rink and was a name synonymous with hockey. I was a traditionalist and was very upset that we lost the name but saw it as a new start. Of course, I still had doubts on whether it would succeed, but was prepared to give it a go.

I don't know whether it was because the players felt the rug may be pulled at any moment, or something they put in the tea, but the changing room was great that year. We did really well, competed, and I got a shed load of points.

I contacted Ivan Matulik who I had been drafted with and he agreed to join the club after only one year in the British game. He was a superb player with an incredible skating power and has done well ever since. When you look at that roster, it oozed quality. We had Chris Palmer, Merv Priest (who had played for Romford, Teeside and Milton Keynes during the season), Deano (Dean Edmiston), Mike Ware (with his mandatory 300 penalty minutes), Les Lovell and Paul Pentland as well as Paul Hand and Moray. We were all friends and it was great.

Ivan recently said that 1994/95 season was the best year he had in British hockey and I would agree with him. For some reason it was really fun to play that year and he was great to play along-side. We formed an understanding and scored 374 points between us. However, where he got Stanko Horansky from is anyone's guess! He had apparently played for Czech side Slovan Bratislava. Ivan asked him to come and play for the Racers but we didn't know he had been in a mental hospital and was seriously crazy with lots of issues. He began not to take his medication and he started to do stupid things. Players would ask him to pass the puck and he wouldn't and then he wanted to fight with them in the dressing room. He didn't last too long and was moved on.

Richie Lamb was another good player, now living in Australia, as is Les Lovell who was one of my best friends in the team. Alongside Mike Ware was another complete nutcase, Scott Plews. He got 147 penalty minutes that year and you never knew what he was going to do on the ice. He was good to have in the team and loved to play hockey. In fact, let's be fair to him, he was a thug! He loved to be the 'goon' and really liked piling in. A lot of guys would keep away from him.

The team spirit guided us to the playoff finals and we murdered Nottingham in the semis 11-7, getting them back for a 25-11 aggregate loss in the Benson and Hedges Cup semi-final. I got a hat-trick and three assists in the game and we really thought we could take it into the final and cap an excellent year. Unfortunately, Sheffield beat us up good the day after, 2-7, to take the league and championship double. We had played in the second semi the night before and we were dead on our feet. Some of their players actually laughed at us in that final because we were so out of it. Although it wasn't fair and we gave everything, that's life I suppose.

It wasn't an ideal end to the season but a pretty satisfying one. I had scored 207 points and the top line of Ivan, myself and Chris Palmer was certainly the most potent in the league. We scored 536 points between us and I was also the first player in the league to score 2,000 points – an amazing feeling.

We had got through the playoffs and survived the year and the entire roster was looking forward to a well-earned summer. However, out of the blue, the team folded on 12 June 1995. While I had been worried how a team that had so nearly collapsed the year before could survive, I didn't expect this to come. It turned out that the owners had failed to reach an agreement with Murrayfield Ice Rink on the level of its rent.

If you're hiring out a rink it's tough to balance the books. There's no real income – you don't get the revenue from the vending machines or in the bar unless your contract is very, very good. You can't blame the rinks for this – it is business – but it puts a lot of pressure on the team to diversify its income.

Within days many clubs were tapping me up. I had been married to Melissa for a year and we had just had our first child, Sarah, so I had to consider my options very carefully. I had the chance to go to Fife but in the end decided to go to Sheffield and leave Scotland. Melissa has always supported my decisions but lets me know if she feels something isn't right. She was a 'friend of a friend' who I had met in a bar in Edinburgh a few years before we married. We used to go out in a big group, but she had a boyfriend, and that was that. But after a while, the group became mostly single and we got together. On 27 May 1994 we married at St Mary's church in Edinburgh.

Leaving was a gut-wrenching decision and one of the hardest I had to make. Edinburgh was in my heart. In its favour, Sheffield had the bigger arena as well as Alex Dampier, and I knew some of the players too. They offered me a three-year deal on good money with a car and house, and after I had chatted with Dave Simms and Alex Dampier and also asked Melissa's advice, we decided to go for it.

Fife were Murrayfield's main rivals and the fans hated them, so to go and play for a team I 'hated' wasn't the done thing. I just couldn't do it. I couldn't move to a team I wanted to beat so much! And it was the best decision I ever made.

15

'PERHAPS THE LEAGUE GREW TOO FAST...'

As I was enjoying my first season at my new club, the game underwent one of the biggest changes ever seen in the sport. On 28 November 1995 Superleague was born, creating an all-singing, all-dancing league with fully professional players, 'super venues' and the best quality on the ice.

It was very exciting to be a player when it began. We knew that we were going to be professional and therefore paid well, with the added bonus of compulsory medical insurance, assurances about being released for international duty, although that didn't affect me, as well as playing at some of the best arenas in the country and against some of the best players the sport could offer. Initially, the league was based around seven core teams, although all clubs across the country were invited to join. These were Basingstoke Bison, Cardiff Devils, Durham Wasps, Sheffield Steelers, Bracknell Bees, Guildford Flames and Manchester Storm.

However, within five months Durham had dropped out as their rink shut in July 1996 and the Nottingham Panthers and Ayr Scottish Eagles took their place. Losing Durham was very sad as they were really successful, with a great pedigree, but within a year they were replaced by Newcastle Cobras, owned by Sir John Hall who was the chair of Newcastle United FC, in the region.

It could have been any of the clubs but, backed by a wealthy owner, Newcastle competing in the league really shook up hockey and the finance of the sport. With no disrespect to Sir John, and teams like Manchester, the way they operated with a 'win all' player recruitment policy really pumped the prices up for other clubs who then struggled to match them. Some guys were on £50,000 a year and they were awful. No other team could compete with that. Because of the money Newcastle had behind them, and the fact that Rick Brebant was player/coach, they could attract big players and they did throw money around to get them. It sounded good at the time and I'm sure the fans up there loved it, but other teams had to pick up the pieces.

This is what people do not understand about sport. In my view, if you're spending money to compete against other teams and you're in it for the long haul, then it's different. But if you're in it for a few years and you can put what you want it into it, especially people as wealthy as John Hall, it creates problems. Other teams panic and try and compete, otherwise they may lose their sponsors and crowds. They start to chase the golden egg. Some teams could afford to spend £1 million and others £300,000. But when the backers leave, the bottom falls out and the club as well as fans suffer. And the last thing the league needed was for teams to drop out – especially with sponsorship from Sekonda and extensive satellite television coverage coming in later years.

Understandably, criteria for entry to the Superleague were based on finance, commitment to junior hockey and marketing as well as the quality of players and venue. Member teams had to invest a share capital of £10,000 with the league and upgrade their facilities to hold 2,000 seats in the first year, 3,000 by the third and finally 5,000 in the fifth. They also had to look at installing lighting for television purposes. The league was based on the premise of no promotion or relegation but the real key was who made up the rosters. A squad had to have seventeen full-time players and most clubs looked to imports.

This angered several clubs and Fife, who had submitted an application to join the league, withdrew after their rink manager John Brady declared the aim to use all-import sides to be immoral. On the other side of the coin, Guildford also pulled out when they failed to win promotion and persuade their rink's owners to increase the capacity from 2,200.

Yet in the first year the result was a very strong league with the top teams attracting high numbers of fans and therefore improving their bargaining power with the governing body. The teams effectively took over the league and began running things the way they wanted it to be run.

With hindsight, following the demise of the league in 2003, you can see it was flawed from the beginning. But all owners believed in the model. In every business you have to plan for five years and setting share capital and expected venue capacity rises like that were in good faith and with good intentions.

The league was trying to get away from rinks like Lee Valley – the smaller venues where there's no seating – and looked for real arena teams. They were trying to build something. I could see where they were coming from and the guys behind it were very smart and believed they could achieve it. But in the same breath there weren't a lot of venues that could expand to create the size of rink the league wanted, nor were there enough teams that had the financial clout to attract players and thereby fill their venues.

Personally, I think the league didn't believe that some teams would drop out so quickly, or that it could end with just five teams in 2003. Perhaps the Superleague grew too fast and the teams spent too much money. Who knows? But in the end it just didn't work.

As for the import levels, I could see where John Brady was coming from. When the rules said that there was no restriction on the number of players you could bring in from overseas there was a big uproar. I think perhaps some owners thought that if they saturated the market with imported players it would bring the salaries down in general because those players were cheaper. Whoever thought that must have been out of their minds! Sure, to a certain extent it would have, but teams wanted to win and would do it with large rosters and big name players. So you could have saturated the market, but these teams were paying big money for the same players anyway because they wanted to win and keep the fans coming in through the door. It never made economic sense to do that, but they decided that was the route they wanted to take.

Also, I believe they wanted to get away from the idea that the British players were making a lot of money. Home-grown players wanted to push up their salaries before Superleague because if you had five imports the Brits became very important to the success of the team. I really understood this and the clubs wanted to reduce the salaries.

But even now the teams at the top still want to win and will do anything for that to happen. They cannot sacrifice winning in order to satisfy other aims like increasing the number of British players. And they certainly won't do it because one venue is attracting 500 people while they are getting 7,000.

It meant that a lot of British players and kids of around sixteen to eighteen years old packed the sport in. There was a survey done recently that showed only two of the kids that had played in the GB Under-19 gold medal-winning team in 2003/04 still played. That is certainly not how you should grow your sport. You can look at it far down the road and objectively, but if you look at it seriously, no business can survive with imported talent or employment.

At present we have ten imports per team in the Elite League. That's 100 players across the league and therefore 100 lots of paperwork. It all adds up. I just cannot see the logic in that. This is exactly what happened in Superleague, and in the end that fell through. It leaves you wondering if the current teams will have to change their business models in the future to sustain the league?

Despite the great players that came over and the standard of hockey that ensued, fans loved to see the British kids flying around the ice, scoring, fighting, you name it. When I coached Belfast Giants, the spectators loved to watch Marc Levers and Mark Morrison as well as our British back-up netminder playing and by god, did they go nuts when one of them scored. The fans wanted them to do well and loved it when I put them out on the ice. I think in Superleague we got away from looking at what the fans wanted – yes, they wanted quality hockey, but they wanted to see the Brits play as well. But on the other hand, I know that the British players were their own worst enemies by asking for too much and the owners didn't want to give them the power to dictate their salaries.

If you looked at the British players who made a real difference in the seasons before Superleague – and I'm talking about the same sort of impact an import would have had – if those players were to leave their club it was a real blow to the side and its aspirations. In the end, increasing import levels meant that clubs didn't rely on these 'make a difference' Brits, who were asking for high salaries. It also meant that the Brits had to lower their demands, and that's what the clubs wanted.

Despite the loss of some British talent, what the league did was create 'super arenas' and the biggest one of all was the 17,500-seater Nynex Arena up in Manchester. Before Manchester Storm joined the top flight, they were regularly attracting 10,000 fans to watch Division One games against local rivals Blackburn. I say local rivals – this was a new team so hadn't had the chance to create a rivalry! That was phenomenal. It meant that the sport had a real success story, something the national press picked up on, and we all wanted to play there. A couple of years later it attracted the highest European indoor ice hockey attendance.

When it went belly up a few years later I think we missed a real trick as a sport. Whoever was in charge at the time should now look at themselves in the mirror and ask what they did to turn it the other way. Over a few years crowds went from 15,000 to 5,000. When they folded, Storm had an average crowd of around 2,500. For that to have happened there has to have been something wrong with the people making the decisions. Manchester was a beacon for us all to follow, and to get to that level was incredible, but then to lose it… questions need to be answered.

It should never have happened but I suppose I will never know the real reason why it did. Perhaps there were too many free tickets, I don't know. But when it did happen it should have been a warning sign for the league. The Arena and the Storm created their own hype and the crowds weren't turning up to watch top-notch hockey, they came for the entertainment and identified with the players. You didn't need five NHLers at that time to attract five-figure crowds and despite the recent influx of top-calibre players we can't get those sort of crowds now.

As a player, it was amazing to play at the Nynex Arena and no one could quite believe what they were coming into when they skated on the ice. I thought Sheffield's new arena was excellent but the Nynex, later renamed the MEN (*Manchester Evening News*) just dwarfed it. It was incredible but unfortunately will probably never happen again.

One thing that did spoil the league was the lack of promotion and relegation. I am a firm believer that you have to play for something. Towards the later days of Superleague we were playing basically to keep the league alive and financially 'sound'. In my view you need to make sure the players, fans and sponsors are not cheated. Sport should be exciting and there needs to be something on the line. If every team makes the playoffs or the same teams play in the same league every year then where is the pressure? Where do the team, management and fans get the boost and that 'push' to go forward? You are just surviving. If you are not making changes, then you stagnate and that's something the league did towards the end, so it's no wonder the fans turned off. Perhaps the people in charge should have got together with other leagues to create something but that's another story.

While towards the end of a season the fans may think there is nothing to play for I can ensure them that hockey players love to play even when there is little on the line. Belfast played Cardiff in the last game of the season after we had been knocked out in the championship and I was genuinely pissed off when the guys cocked up! We love to win and love to play.

The NHL is currently trying to change the rules and look at anything to keep it real and up to date. Our attraction is to get tough guys in to fight and that's it. Yes, it does put bums on seats but for how long? Perhaps we should look at making the blue lines bigger – from six to twelve inches so the margin of error goes up. Perhaps we could stop the goalies coming out? We don't seem to do anything in this country yet hope the fans will continue to show up. That's a dangerous game.

16

'A GREAT WAY TO SECURE THE GRAND SLAM...'

Moving out of Scotland for the first time was always going to be nerve racking and seeing the quality of players Sheffield Steelers had on the roster was quite frightening. I had grown up with most of the players at Edinburgh and looking around a new dressing room at guys such as Steve Nemeth and Ken Priestlay meant I was a little apprehensive.

Coach Alex Dampier realised he needed some fresh blood in there and the squad underwent a massive influx of players. He tried to develop a team that was the best in the country but also one with a balance of British players and imports. He believed this would promote the game to the people of Sheffield. In the roster it meant that some of the older guys left the club because they were concerned about becoming third-liners. I have to admit it took me a while to settle at first but after a short time I loved every minute. And I couldn't have asked for a better debut, scoring five against Swindon.

In Sheffield there were two sides to the dressing room. On one there was myself, Tim Cranston, Nicky Chinn, Martin McKay and later David Longstaff, all of whom had a laugh and shared a joke. The other side was really serious and straight-laced with Steve Nemeth and Ron Shudra among others, and we used to wind them up all the time. Good natured of course. We always had a go at people and it really bonded the whole team together. In fact, I'm sure that was one of the reasons we did so well that year.

Shudra copped it a lot. He may have been slowing down back then, like me, but he was a class act and really sharp. We used to say to him that this was his last game and we should take him round the back to shoot him, like you would do a horse: 'We have a field round the back for you Shuds!' It was a really good dressing room. Nemeth struggled with his elbow back then so when he did play he went full out but was clearly injured. I think the club were upset with that. They reckoned it was something he brought over with him and it did cause some resentment between the staff and him. They thought he should have owned up to the injury earlier, but he just wanted to play and, despite the problems, was an amazing player.

Despite all the quality around me I was never concerned for my place in the first line, as long as I didn't relax, kept working and kept on scoring. I was young and in my prime, and I scored 123 points, 25 ahead of Priestlay and 65 in front of Cranston. I also notched my 900th league goal on 26 November against Fife. Looking back, there were some real personalities in that dressing room so I suppose they must have felt some resentment at me doing so well.

The whole club was geared up for success and we certainly did achieve everything we set out to that year. Behind the scenes was Brian English, our team doctor, who is now at Chelsea. He was a brilliant guy who was always testing and pushing himself. He ended up working for the Olympic athletics team. I saw him at the airport recently and we had a really good chat, but he never mentioned Chelsea so you could imagine my surprise when I saw him on the TV carrying off one of their players! He was a staunch Chelsea fan and used to try and see them as much as he could so I suppose he landed on his feet.

Another reason Sheffield were going places was the fans. I cannot describe how passionate they were. They would raise the roof when you played and I remember the rink installing an extra 1,000 seats for the visit of Nottingham. By the end of the season, the Panthers certainly began to hate Sheffield!

I had only been there a few weeks when I was involved in a road accident. I was coming back from the golf course with Chris Kelland and Scott Neil who was driving. Scott started to check something out, either looking for a tape or something and we careered off the road (he would later blame me, even though I wasn't driving).

We were lucky there wasn't something coming the other way or we wouldn't have been here now. We cut across the road, through the central reservation and suddenly a hedge came towards us. I thought we would be okay, but there was a massive drop on the other side, so the car hit the hedge and flipped onto the roof. Kelland was in real pain in the back seats as he was screaming and Scott was knocked out. The windows were smashed and I managed to exit to pull out Chris. He was okay, though really sore, but Scott was halfway out when I got round to him. I pulled him from the car and he managed to regain consciousness. When he did, the first thing he did was to check if his teeth were still intact in the side mirror! His car was only thirty miles old and brand new, so of course he was a little upset. The medics sorted us out but Scot was all over the place – he didn't know what day it was, literally. He was concussed. I think it affected Scott for a long time afterwards. Even on the ice he didn't really know what was going on.

He claimed I grabbed the steering wheel, but Chris backed up the fact that I had shouted at Scott because a bend was coming up. It was very scary indeed. We played Nottingham the day after and I was awful because I was really shaken up. Clyde Tuyl wanted us not to play, but we did and perhaps it was a bad idea. Clyde was another reason the club was strong. A real good guy but very quiet who would spend twenty-four hours a day in the office driving the team forward.

Another rock in the backroom is the legend that is Dave Simms. I didn't know Dave when I joined, but I certainly know him now, as does the rest of the sport! Simmsy was the guy who softened people up to join the club. He would tell you how good the club was, then Dampier would make contact, followed by Steve Crowther. Back then it was all done through lawyers because no one knew who held my registration after the collapse of the Racers.

Simmsy loves the Steelers and I'm sure he would sleep with them all if he could. He holds the Steelers close to his heart and he is the heartbeat and soul of that club. Although he may be a little bit swayed because of that desire, I think he is great for British ice hockey. You need someone controversial and ready to cause a stir as well as someone who isn't worried about speaking out and Dave is that someone. He may speak out of turn, but he isn't bothered. Dave once went to a meeting representing the Steelers and the guy from Manchester said, 'Don't bother speaking Simmsy, we know what you are going to say.' It turned out Simmsy had put his comments in the paper a couple of days before!

The Sheffield-Nottingham rivalry is second to none. Not only do they have bench-clearing fights, they also love to wind each other up. I was looking on the internet the other day and glanced at the Panthers site. On the front page it had the mock league table on the front for the new season. With no games played Sheffield were on the bottom. Then, on the Sheffield website, their last game result read 'Steelers 99 Nottingham 0'. I think that's brilliant!

Simmsy creates a lot of hype but sometimes he can go too far. He will divulge signings from around the league days before the teams have a chance to announce it themselves. If he hears someone is joining another club he will get it on his website straightaway. And he can never understand why some players don't want to play for Sheffield. If a player wants to move clubs and they have spoken to the Steelers, for Simmsy it is a done deal and he does not understand if they then go and sign for another team.

He's certainly getting worse with age and loves to wind Nottingham up even more these days. The Panthers once accused the Steelers of breaking the wage cap and he said, 'At least when we were breaking it, we won something. You break it and you win sod all. When we cheat we win!' Comments like that haven't won him many friends and he and Panthers' manager Gary Moran do not speak at all.

Anyway, as if the car crash wasn't enough, I had been in Sheffield about a month when somebody tried to break into my house. Melissa had left the keys in the door and I couldn't find them. The neighbour had seen two guys at the front door so I knew they had been taken. Luckily, I owned a Rottweiler at the time. I knew they would be back and I caught them round the corner on the way to my house so I got hold of one of them, but the police said I couldn't do anything as they weren't inside my house. It was certainly an interesting start to life in Sheffield.

As the year progressed we all felt something special was on the cards. While we never expected to achieve what we did, we knew we were a good side. Perhaps not the greatest team, but certainly the best collection of individual talent in the league. In the end we won the Grand Slam and I finished top of the scoring charts once again. There were a lot of good players in the league that year and I went in to try my best. But the team I had around me was fantastic and the top line of myself, Tommy Plommer and Ken clicked, as it did when it was varied with other players such as Scott. More than 8,500 people were turning up for the games on average at the arena and they lifted us all year. We never thought we would lose and in fact we only lost 4 times, taking the last 10 matches to win the league title.

My European experience with the Racers certainly helped us to get further than any other British team when we played in the European Cup in Holland. It was a great tour and the following we took over was really amazing. It was good for the players to get away from the same ice and play together. We never knew what to expect and we were unlucky not to get through. Played in October 1995, we beat the Tilburg Trappers (Holland) 4-1, lost to Olympia Ljubjana (Slovenia) 3-5 and hammered Txuri-Urdin (Spain) 9-2. The loss to Ljubjana was key, but we just couldn't get back in it despite pulling it back to 3-4. I was also named Player of the Tournament.

While the loss was disappointing, we came back with loads of confidence and grew in stature throughout the rest of the season. On 2 December we reached the Benson & Hedges Cup final at our home arena after scraping through against Fife in the semis. An astonishing 10,136 people packed into the arena as we faced Nottingham and we felt if we were going to be beaten, it would only be in a one-off cup game like this one.

1 *Right:* A young-looking Murrayfield number 9!

2 *Below:* Playing for Great Britain was a highlight of my career.

3 Left: Licensed to thrill… the things Simmsy had me doing at Sheffield. This shot announced my signing. (Bob Westerdale)

4 Below: Playing for Sheffield at Manchester's Nynex Arena. More than 10,000 fans would regularly pack the place.

5 I had some great years at Sheffield, especially winning the Grand Slam.

6 Now with Chelsea FC, then Sheffield doctor Brian English gives me the low-down.

7 A charity racing day with Sheffield.

8 Above: I spent two years at the Ayr
Scottish Eagles. (Ronnie Nichol)

9 Right: Promotional shot for Sheffield
Steelers

10 Getting whacked up against the boards at Dundee.

11 Watching my Dundee charges from the bench.

12 *Above:* Watch it! The scene after my fight with Coventry's Gareth Owen in 2001. Little did I know that two minutes later an incident would leave me facing a charge of assault. (Mark Tredgold)

13 *Right:* Being player/coach at Edinburgh was certainly frustrating at times. (Tony Boot)

14 Watching the play develop. (Tony Boot)

15 Picking a player out. (Tony Boot)

16 *Above:* I have always been a
playmaker and prided myself
on my ability to see the play.
(Tony Boot)

17 *Right:* Just before
the National Anthem at
Edinburgh in 2005. I use this
time to think about the game
ahead and stay focused. (Tony
Boot)

18 My kids Paul and Sarah before my trip to meet the Queen.

19 Melissa and I at Holyrood.

20 Receiving the MBE. The Queen was great and put me at ease.

21 Icing for Great Britain against Denmark.

22 *Above:* Just missing the net for Great Britain against Denmark.

23 *Left:* Paul Thompson's testimonial in 2005. (Tony Boot)

24 'Arrested' during Thommo's testimonial. (Mark Tredgold)

25 The Elite Coaches in 2005. From left to right: myself (Belfast), Paul Heavey (Sheffield), Paul Thompson (Coventry), Mark Bernard (Basingstoke), Paul Adey (Nottingham) and an unusually shy Dennis Maxwell (London). (Mark Tredgold)

26 *Above:* Creating the space to play in. (Tony Boot)

27 *Left:* Watching the guys warm up in Belfast. (Tony Boot)

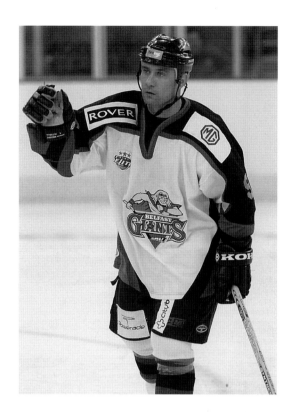

28 Line change signal. (Tony Boot)

29 Face-off. (Tony Boot)

30 Left: Watching the game from the bench and taking a breather. (Tony Boot)

31 Below: With owner Neil Morris to announce my signing as Manchester Phoenix player-coach. (Mike Appleton)

Truthfully, we had been slightly lucky to get there. Fife surprised us in the semi. Back in Sheffield for the second leg, Fife's Ian Robertson shot from point and it flew through Wayne Cowley – this frightened us. We threw everything at them and we sneaked through in overtime through my sudden-death winner. We had come back three times and they worked their bag off, so we were lucky to get away with that one.

The final was nip and tuck all the way. We were one up at the end of the first until the game changed on its head in the second. As we pushed ahead on another powerplay, the Panthers relaxed and, with a couple of seconds left to kill, Chuck Taylor went over to clear but was checked by Ken Priestlay. I picked the puck up and for some reason the Panthers stood off me. I drifted behind the net but at the last moment dropped back in front of their netminder and poked it into the goal. There was real daylight between us. We then scored again through Plommer on our very next shot and some forty seconds later I robbed the puck from Chuck and made a dash for the corner, drifted to the point of the goal-line and knocked it into the top corner from an acute angle.

They pulled back two but I notched an empty netter at the end where I hit the water bottle on the net. Yes, it was showboating and a little cocky. My second was something I prided myself on. I used to drift to the goal-line and scoop it in top shelf. I always aimed for the goalie's shorts because they used to lose their angles.

A couple of weeks later on 16 December an innocuous game against Durham at Sunderland certainly attracted some unwanted attention. Although the game finished 6-6, it will be remembered for a thirty-five-minute brawl that saw myself and several other players spend some serious time in the penalty box after Chinny (Nicky Chinn) caught Durham's Ross Lambert with his stick.

I was on the ice at the time. Behind me, out of the corner of my eye, I saw a guy go down, and then Chinny went past me with the puck and nearly scored. The next thing I knew, Dale Lambert, Ross's brother, had jumped off the bench onto the ice and tried to take Chinny's head off. I thought, 'What the hell is going on here?' Suddenly, everyone dropped the gloves and it went off. We all wrestled around and there were punches thrown from all angles. When it calmed down, around half an hour later, someone said that Ross had lost his eye, which really shocked me.

Ross went off for treatment but came back on after a minute and you could his eye was a mess and he couldn't see. But he began wielding his stick like a hatchet and looking for Chinny. In the meantime, I had been kicked out of the game and given a match penalty, really for doing nothing. I never actually did anything that bad, just wrestled about with Dale, but then again, there were bodies everywhere so it could have been any Durham player. If Chinny had caught him with a stick, he deserved to have his head taken off. Later, I was in the dressing room with Chinny and the police came in and arrested him.

A few months later we all ended up in Leeds Crown Court for a jury trial and to be honest we all hadn't a clue what was going on. Chinny certainly could have gone to jail and was up for something like Actual Bodily Harm. When the foreman read the verdict: 'Not guilty', we all cheered and got rollicked by the judge. It was an emotional moment. I actually had a tear in my eye because the pressure on Chinny was immense. Looking back, I don't think he meant to do it, and Ross's eye was okay in the end. Chinny lifted his stick up and caught the guy. It was never even given as a penalty by the referee.

That sort of incident with players going to court because of their on-ice actions will happen more often and I think it is wrong. Don't get me wrong; if someone takes a liberty with someone and it goes beyond the boundaries then they should be in court. If someone comes around and hits someone from behind like Vancouver Canucks' Todd Bertuzzi did in the NHL, you cannot allow that to happen and have to put a stop to it. If someone is 6ft 5ins and goes after someone who doesn't want to fight and then he just sucker-punches him, then you have to do something. There has to be a code of conduct.

I think the referees have a big role to play in this but they are inconsistent. Guys like Moray Hanson are excellent at spotting trouble and putting a stop to it, but also letting the fight go. You can tell they work hard. But there are some who don't and the chief referee doesn't back them.

Bertuzzi's attack was a blatant assault. He broke Steve Moore's neck in a game between the Canucks and the Colorado Avalanche by clattering him from behind. I'm sure he feels really bad about it now. Perhaps he was pumped up too much, because it was the heat of the moment and a playoff game. That incident was on the news all over the world but I have seen a worse one. In 1997, I saw Carmine Vani two-hand Scott Allison over the head with a stick during a game. It hit him right across the shoulder and head and it could have killed him. It takes a different type of person to do that and is beyond the usual tough-guy status. People think these guys are idiots and the players will not tolerate those sorts of actions.

Chinny was lucky not to go to prison, but the verdict made us stronger as a team and again we kicked on. Securing the league title by beating Nottingham 7-2 we headed into the playoffs.

The group series didn't start so well, with a loss to the Basingstoke Bison, but we smacked Fife 11-0, then tonked Nottingham, beat Fife at home and lost away at Nottingham before the series was rounded off with a 7-3 win against the Bison to reach Wembley. After breezing through the semi 6-3 against Humberside Hawks, we again faced old foes Nottingham in the final. Cruising at 3-0 after twenty-two minutes, the Panthers scored three in ninety-four seconds with the final period scoreless. Overtime couldn't separate us either.

I always knew it would come round again. A shootout. After my disaster against Cardiff I prayed hard that I wouldn't need to take one. The shootout was really tense with Nottingham missing through Paul Adey before we took the lead with Andre Malo. Mike Blaisdell scored for them to make it 1-1 before, four missed penalties later, Rob Wilson slotted his in. I knew if Darren Durdle scored his for the Panthers I would be up next. As he fired his shot Wayne Cowley got everything in front and saved it with ease. I went mental. Of course, I would have loved this chance to redeem myself but thank god it didn't come. I couldn't have gone through that again.

It is unfair to settle a game like that but it was truly amazing and a great way to secure the Grand Slam. We all piled on Wayne in a wave of adrenaline and relief. At that moment, nothing goes through your mind. I had been on the opposite side watching teams do this and so wanted to enjoy it. And the fact that we had beaten the Panthers to win the league, cup and championship made the fans party that little bit more.

The celebrations continued all the way to Sheffield and we got a police escort to the arena in an open-top bus, with thousands of fans lining the route home. What a year, one I will never forget.

17

'TO PRODUCE ONE OF THE FINEST PERFORMANCES THE CLUB HAS SEEN...'

Nobody really knew what to expect with Superleague but one thing was for sure: all member clubs were spending vast sums and the rosters around the country looked pretty scary.

The league itself was launched at the Sports Café in London in September 1996, while some players self-consciously rollerbladed around Trafalgar Square. The things the league bosses come up with – thank god they didn't ask me! In Sheffield we wanted to build on the Grand Slam the year before and the club was very ambitious. We kept most of the existing line-up, with Priestlay, Cranston and myself re-signing alongside David Longstaff, Rob Wilson and Andrew Malo, and we brought in Jamie Leach (drafted by Pittsburgh Penguins in 1987) from Rochester Americans (AHL), Cape-Breton Oilers' Frank Kovacs (drafted by Minnesota North Stars in 1990) and Jason Lafreniere (drafted by Quebec Nordiques in 1985) from Austrian side Villach VSV.

Jamie was hardworking and a real grinder and came over with the reputation of being a goalscorer. Frank Kovacs had a big rep for dropping the gloves, and was signed as an enforcer. But he was one of those guys who would be tough with the 'normal' guys but not the 'heavyweights'. This disappointed the team as he was more of a guy that came in and slung them around with the smaller chaps.

Coach Alex Dampier put myself, Ken and Cranston on the top line, but to freshen it up in a league that was really burgeoning quality wise, he rotated it with some of the other forwards. On D in the first line was a Corey Beaulieu, a great kid but one of the dirtiest players I have seen in the UK. He would and hurt some guys pretty bad – especially a couple of guys from Ayr and Basingstoke's Darren Hurley too. A Manchester player wouldn't forget him in a hurry too after he broke three fingers on one of his hands! He was really fearless, but a good guy. Despite our ribbing Shuds (Ron Shudra) hung around too – proving he is one of the most consistent guys in this country. He is the sort of player I would want in my roster as he handles the puck really well, is a great passer and controls the powerplay. Okay, his skating wasn't fantastic, but he always got the job done.

After nine games of the season I hadn't scored and I started to get worried. We knew the league was of a much better standard but it took some time to gel the team together. If you look at everyone's scoring that season you'll see how much the standard had improved – especially with the goaltenders. I got 45 points, with Priestlay in second on 37, and no one really had what you would class as a great year.

It was a culture shock and tough to get used to. I almost had to relearn how to play the game, re-evaluate how I defended and learn not to get downhearted if I wasn't scoring or setting up from all angles. That was the way the league went. Manchester Storm were very strong, as were Nottingham and Cardiff, so Sheffield had to step up. In truth, the organisers had got the league they wanted – an international league with all teams competing and capable of beating each other on any particular night. Crowds were in excess of 10,000 at Manchester and the Steelers averaged around 7,000.

Having won the league the year before, we were invited to take part in the European Cup, a competition that some said was losing its relevance because of the major difference in the quality of the teams across the continent. But we first had to qualify through a tricky group on home ice in October. Every player played his part as we cruised the group with 3 wins from 3. We crushed Hielo Jaca 16-0, Tilburg 5-1 and Bucharest 4-1 as they had no match for our power. It meant the team heading over to Hameenlinna in Finland for the semi-finals.

Our first game was against Storhamar and we competed well, just losing 7-5 after being 4-2 up after two periods. Cranston said that we were refereed out of the game and he may have been right. But we got a great start and never capitalised. The second match, on 16 November, saw us get our first point. Before the game, hosts Hameenlinna were warming up and we were watching them and I uttered an audible obscenity and said that we were going to get killed. Sometimes you can just tell by the way a team is practising that they are head and shoulders above you.

To be fair, we should have been killed. We had Nemeth out and they were top of the Finnish league. Yet we raised our game to produce one of the finest performances the club has seen. It finished 2-2 and in the last period we hammered them but could not score. Realistically our chances were gone and we lost 5-4 to Novopolotsk the day after.

After the drawn game some of the players went out for a few beers to celebrate in the local area and were involved in a bit of a brawl. Apparently, although I was in bed at the time, netminder Jimmy Hibbert took some stick from some Norwegian fans and several blows were exchanged. Everyone was pretty hammered, but it certainly didn't take our guys that long to get wound up. Jamie van der Horst was the central character in this. I was told that he had calmed things down in his own style (he used to be a bouncer) and some of the fans had got hurt pretty badly. Jamie was a belting player but was insecure about how he played. He was always getting ribbed because of his stocky frame, but he was strong as an ox and he was conscious of it.

Apparently the police got involved and when I was woken up by Dave Simms the next morning he had the longest face ever. I thought someone had died. He was distraught. Luckily nothing came of it.

With 3 goals and 3 assists at the end of the tournament I was named Most Valuable Player. I was also asked to stay and play in Finland with Hameenlinna. I wanted to meet with the general manager before I decided anything so I had a chat with him. But as I did, Alex Dampier came around the corner to make a phone call and saw what I was up to. I think he realised something was going on. I had signed for a full season with Sheffield and was going to honour that but I asked them about next year to see what was on the go. I felt bad because Damps had come in and caught me speaking to the other team but I never took their offer anyway.

I must mention that this sort of thing happens in hockey all the time. All players are always looking at their options and if a team wants to speak to them, they would be daft not to hear what they had to say. It doesn't mean they're off on the next flight. It means they can make choices at the end of a season.

Around the same time I was named on the BIHA's list of Great Britain players but I declined to take part. My reasons for this have been covered already but Peter Woods, the coach at the time, said after they had failed to qualify for the Olympics that it was not his aging GB side that had let him down but 'the Brits who stuck two fingers up to the national programme.'

I was annoyed at this because my reasons for not returning were clear. It was too amateurish and Great Britain was paying some players to play for the team and that's why some of the British players did not want to know. I'm sure if I asked for money I would have got it. I still wouldn't have returned out of principle though.

We came back from the European Championships a closer unit and really kicked on to complete the season in style. The Grand Slam was a distant memory and everyone wanted to improve. We finished second behind Cardiff in the league and blasted all in front of us once more to take the playoffs. Although I never played that well, concentrating on playing smart defence, Jamie Leach and Jason Lafreniere really stepped up for us. The American players always peaked at the end of the season, as their leagues are set up for the playoffs.

Up until the playoffs I had had a pretty decent year. In the B&H Cup (Steelers went out at the semi stage to Nottingham) I scored 22 points from 10 games. In the league I finished with 45 (13 goals and 32 assists) from 41. I also scored 9 from 8 in the playoff group stages.

Before the playoffs got underway, some bright spark decided to change the rules once again for overtime. The ISL officials stated that if a winner has not been established after five minutes of overtime, one player from each side would be withdrawn for a further five-minute period. The system would continue until only three players and the goalie remain on the ice. They would play for further five-minute periods until a result is decided. Why stop there? Why not 0 on 0 and let the keepers thwack it out!

I think they wanted to do away with penalty shots but it was a real farce and, as sod's law would have it, the first game between Nottingham and Ayr took more than four and a half hours to complete! Changing rules is a disease in British hockey. I've been in games where the refs have had to contact the heads of the league to find out what the rules are. The 2004 Crossover competition was a prime example. The BNL had ten minutes for overtime and the Elite had five...

Anyway, turning over Cardiff 5-2 in the semi showed we meant business. Cardiff's coach reckoned that we were all diving everywhere but we dominated from start to finish. Isn't it true that any penalties are always the opposing team's fault? No coach would send his team out to dive, it just wouldn't happen. A week later we took on Nottingham (yet again) at a packed Nynex Arena in Manchester with 14,116 seeing us take the game 3-1. The final was amazing and the place was buzzing. Lafreniere was awesome and netted a superb goal.

It was another perfect end to the year although the future of the club was a little uncertain. Back in October 1996 it had been put up for sale for £4 million, and some of the franchise was sold to Leeds United FC, who had set up Leeds Ice Hockey Club. Owner George Dodds said that, despite the Grand Slam, the organisation couldn't stand still. He said that the new Superleague would drive costs higher and that investment was needed to maintain the club's position at the front of the sport. Only time would tell.

18

'HE GAVE YOU A BEER FOR BEING GOOD...'

With the club seemingly on a better financial footing, everyone was looking forward to the 1997/98 season. We had finished the previous one in style and wanted to taste success again.

Yet for some reason we didn't recruit well at all and it was a really dismal year. If you took a look at the roster you would see that we had got older as a team but hadn't brought in that many new faces. We needed new blood – and exciting blood. Of course, we had a good list of players who could compete, but there wasn't enough turnover of players to match the rosters of Cardiff, Manchester and others. What the club did was recruit from the current pool of players in the league itself and not from 'overseas' and other leagues.

As a team we had got too used to the set-up and too used to each other, and I include myself in that. Back in Murrayfield we could get away with keeping the roster virtually the same, but now, because the league's teams were improving, we had to as well. And we failed to do that and really got left behind. We had a good team with the mental and physical toughness, but we got stale. Training got too similar. Our goaltending wasn't up to it.

We did recruit Dion Del Monte from Nurenberg Ice Tigers in Germany to improve our goalscoring ratio and Mike Ware came in to add some steel on the D, but it wasn't enough and we finished a poor fourth behind Ayr, Manchester and Bracknell, winning 20 and losing 18. The fans took it really hard, as did the team. We failed to make the playoffs in Manchester and lost to Cardiff Devils in the quarter-finals of the Challenge Cup and to Bracknell Bees in the semi-finals of the Express Cup. Alex Dampier and Clyde Tuyl were moved on as a result.

On 23 February 1997, however, I was part of something great at the club. We knew travelling across the Pennines that the game at the Nynex against Manchester Storm would be good, but we never expected to be part of history. On that night we lost 4-2 but 17,245 packed into the venue to break the record for the highest European indoor attendance at a hockey game. It was incredible and when we first went out on the ice in complete darkness (with Manchester warming up the crowd) it made the hairs stand up on the back of my neck. Every goal Manchester scored was welcomed with a deafening roar. It was a real shame that it didn't last up there.

In that season, Anschutz, one of the largest sporting firms in the world who also owned the LA Kings, formed London Knights. Although they didn't get off to the greatest start a year later, finishing bottom, the move was a big thing for hockey in Britain. Playing out of the Docklands Arena was superb as it was a top-class venue for fans and players and Anschutz had a roster for success. I always remember London coming up to Sheffield and someone tipped me off that they had signed Troy Crowder, a real NHL nutcase. He was drafted by the New Jersey Devils in 1986 and was known for taking no prisoners. He was that tough no one would go near him. When I told the rest of the guys in the dressing room, no one believed me. They were paying him a fortune with rumours ranging from £1,400 to £1,600 a week. When we skated out all the players were craning their necks to see the London line-up and, sure enough, he was there. I'm sure some faces went white on our team.

London folded in 2002 after winning the playoffs in 2000, but some of their set-up was wrong from the start. At first, most of their players were staying in Milton Keynes and travelling for the best part of two and a half hours to get to the arena. Anschutz pulled the plug because they expected to see some return and didn't. We knew they were serious players in the league and that they had a good roster, but the fans started going at first, then stopped, and Anschutz saw no reason to sustain the team.

It was another lost opportunity for the sport in Britain. Although it would've cost them a fortune to play at the rink, the league needed a team in the capital. Why the fans stopped going I will never know. It was dear to watch hockey there and perhaps they weren't seeing enough wins. Perhaps the capital has too many football teams competing for business or the owners expected the Canadian and American people in London to turn up to watch NHL-style hockey. Who knows? But it never seemed to attract the crowds that capital hockey deserves. It wasn't through lack of trying though. You could see where the owners were coming from with their marketing plans and they did a lot of work in schools.

Although the Knights are now defunct or have hibernated depending on if you believe they will reform again to play at the Millennium Dome – one of the sport's greatest rumours – I would love to see the London Racers get a new rink now they have left Lee Valley. It is ridiculous that a conurbation as large as London does not have a decent enough rink to support ice hockey. They pulled out of the Elite League in 2005 because of health and safety concerns at the rink. Lee Valley was a real shed. You couldn't get into the dressing room because it was really small and you had to get changed in the corridor. You have to admire Roger Black for sticking at it so long. He is one of the most passionate people for the sport I have met.

Before the Racers pulled out, I said that it was impossible for them to play out of Lee Valley in the long term at Elite level and I was proved right. The venue was just not up to the job. The Elite League does need a team in the capital, but not at the detriment of the other teams. Each team has to stand on its own two feet. I understand the league will help out various teams, but that cannot be done in the long term. The league needs teams in there but they have to be independent. I can understand if a team loses its sponsor that it may need some help but I would hate to think that in five years' time that the same team is still being supported by the league. What London Racers lacked in terms of overall quality, the Knights had in abundance but they failed to get going in their first season.

For Sheffield, 1998/99 was entertaining to say the least. Before we got under way, George Dodds and Simmsy appointed Don McKee as our new coach. Born in Toronto, Don had been used to coaching college and university players at the University of Waterloo Warriors in Canada for fifteen years before the club asked him to step into the breach. He had an unbelievable hockey brain and he lived for the game. It was his family and life. But in that league you needed to know the players and know the teams and Don had come up against guys with families, ones who had been professional for a number of years and we never really took to his way.

This wasn't because he was a bad coach; it was that his style of coaching didn't suit the hockey in Britain. We had to skate round with tyres in training when we lost and the other teams used to rib us all the time for it. He would also make us practise without pucks. The older chaps never really responded to it, but the youngsters did. He had a new practice everyday and he was really organised – probably the most organised I have ever seen – but sometimes it was over the top. There were meetings after meetings and on our days off he would get us down the rink to see what was going on. We were on top of each other all the time. I have to say that I learnt a lot from him, but it was tough for him to come in without any experience in this league.

In my view, and I'm sure most players will agree, you do not need to be skating every day of the week. Guys just wanted to play and if they lost they knew why and didn't need to be skating harder and harder in practice. Our skating was never the issue. He gave you a beer for being good. It was like a teacher-and-pupil scenario.

We didn't take to it at all and most of the team got pissed off because of the schoolboy stuff. We also went to Russia to take part in the Continental Cup in October 1998, which was one of the biggest mistakes Sheffield has ever made. Simmsy announced our acceptance of the invitation to play in his usual style: 'To travel to Russia and play against the cream of European opposition is like a dream come true.' In reality, it was far from it.

The competition was based in Omsk, some 1,500 miles the other side of Moscow, and it put far too much pressure on the players. We had to get jabs for yellow fever among other things and the travel as well as the accommodation was a nightmare. We flew for four hours to Kiev, then another four to arrive at an absolute shithole with dogs running around in packs outside. We didn't eat or drink right, got our arses kicked every night and two of our guys ended up in hospital with a mystery illness, which they thought might be life threatening, when they returned home. According to the press, the travel alone cost the club something like £13,000.

On that trip we faced Kazakhstan Champions Torpedo, which we drew 4-4, Omsk (lost 5-1) and Lada Togliatti (lost 3-1). They were certainly the cream of European hockey and it showed! All the linesmen were Russian and they didn't like the Canadian style of hockey we played. We were penalised for a total of 179 minutes during the three games, with a mass brawl after a cross check on Ed Courtenay against the hosts. Shuds, Jamie van der Horst, Plommer and Rob Wilson were also thrown out in the game against Togliatti.

To add insult to injury, Don wanted us to skate straight off the coach when we got back. You can imagine what was said, but he didn't listen and that was his way. I remember coming home on the bus after being beaten somewhere and we hadn't played that badly. We always had a crate of beer on the coach for the way back if we won so Willy (Rob Wilson) went down to the front to ask Don for the beers. Before we had got on the coach Don had said that we could have a day off the following day, which had stunned us completely as this normally didn't happen. So the lads decided it would be right to have the beers and Willie as captain was nominated to get them. Two minutes later he came back saying, 'We can't have the beers and we've got practice tomorrow.' You can only imagine the ribbing he took for that.

Talking about buses, I remember the controversy around footballers playing cards and losing thousands. We used to play 'snarpels', a game where you needed to look like you had a better hand than you did. We did it to pass time on a long trip and some of the guys were excellent at it. It was never for big money, you lost what you could afford. You only won two or three quid, but it was great fun and despite what some of my former teammates say (mentioning no names, Ed Courtenay), I was certainly the best card player on the coach.

Anyway, the 'beers' incident, was exactly what Don was like. In my view he was a megalomaniac who liked to be in charge all the time. Yet I'm sure some of the players deserved how he treated us, including myself.

We did play some good hockey that year. In the Challenge Cup final we beat Nottingham 4-0 but we never really kicked on from it. Russia was a mess, we got on top of each other in training and I picked up my first injury – a torn cartilage – and didn't play in the playoffs. We each seemed to pick up an injury: Kovacs was out for a while (he only played 12 games), as was Shuds (11), both requiring surgery on knee injuries. On their return from Russia, Kayle Short and Teeder Wynne got glandular fever and looking back I can understand why everyone was concerned – especially as we had all had jabs for all manner of diseases.

Derek Laxdal got hit in January and failed to finish the season because of concussion. In fact, only Dave Longstaff and Ed Courtenay played in every game. The roster was severely depleted throughout the season and despite the club's efforts to bring in scorers, it just didn't happen, although we did pick up third place, beating Manchester Storm 5-2 in the playoffs. Defenceman Craig Chapman came over with a keen eye for goal and he only got two. But Don didn't want these guys to score anyway. He wanted them to play solid D, but when the top guys didn't score the other guys didn't have the confidence to slot it in.

Don's ways didn't just concentrate on the ice though. He was quite 'handy' off it. My son Paul was born in Chesterfield in October

1998. Although people wind me up and say he is Scottish, I am glad he was born in England because of the excellent support we received at Chesterfield Hospital. Recently I asked him who he supports and he said England. That was a real gut-wrencher.

It was hard at first as he wasn't very well so we were in and out of hospital all the time. His eye and ear ducts were blocked so he needed a lot of treatment. He was born really early in the morning and as luck would have it we were playing on the night. Melissa had a long labour; lasting more than ten hours so it's safe to say I got no sleep and was a mess during the game.

For some reason Don took a piece of me in the media on that night and quite rightly I was fuming. I had a lot on my mind and really shouldn't have played. In my view there's a time and a place for this sort of comment. But that was Don: he would use the press all the time for 'motivation'. He told us once that we should all wear skirts because we were that bad. He would also pinpoint individuals in the press. Perhaps that deflected attention from his own poor performance, I don't know, but in my view you shouldn't name players who played poorly in the media. I can be negative as a coach, but I wouldn't do it to an individual through the media. That is something that should be done privately.

Towards the end of the season things started to get bad at the club. On the ice we were failing miserably, finishing sixth behind Manchester, Cardiff, Nottingham, Bracknell and Ayr in the league, losing in the Express Cup before going out to Cardiff in the playoffs to set up that win against the Storm. And I managed just 38 points in 36 games. Off the ice was no better. We started not to get paid and you could see the guys with their pay cheques running across the road to the bank at 100 miles an hour to get them cashed on payday. If you were behind a player in the queue there was a possibility that there wouldn't be enough left for you.

We were supposedly going to be bought out by a guy called Terry Smith, who claimed to be the European President of the World Indoor Soccer League. To be completely honest he was a joke and actually had no money to his name. In his first meeting with club officials and the captains he turned up with ripped jeans, a shirt and tie and a food-stained suit jacket. The owners had agreed to sell the team to him and the first thing he wanted to do was cut the players' wages. And he wanted to pay the entire amount in the summer. He didn't come across very professionally. He tried to hold a gun to the players' heads by saying if they didn't accept a cut the team would have to be closed down.

He also had some strong views on housing. He said that only the players themselves were named on the housing contracts so if they were playing away, for instance, the wives were effectively staying at our houses free of charge. He said they were 'stealing' from the club, because they were not supposed to be in the houses and were not named as part of the player's accommodation contract! Many of the players were ready to quit but thankfully he never got his mitts on the club. He said he was going to sign the deal but it never happened. Even before he was to take control he would take money out of the club. He would walk into the club shop and take tracksuits and replica shirts. It was a real mess.

In the end the club went into liquidation, owing £592,528 to the taxman. I was part of the meetings as captain, with the owners, fans and lawyers, but the Inland Revenue wanted all of their money. The fans offered to pay £200,000 but they weren't prepared to listen. I felt really sorry for the fans and their investors. Four years previously we had won the Grand Slam and now we were in this state.

Towards the end of the season Ayr Scottish Eagles' coach Jim Lynch, made me an offer to return to Scotland. I wanted to see what was happening in Sheffield before I made a decision, as I didn't want to run away from a club I held close to my heart. But as the club went under I decided to make the move back north of the border to play at the new Centrum Arena. It was a tough decision as I had fond memories of Sheffield. Thankfully, the fans' efforts were not in vain as local businessman Darren Brown reformed the Steelers six weeks after they had gone under. He owned sixty-five per cent, while fans group Friends of Steelers Hockey owned thirty-three per cent. I was very happy for them.

19

'AGAIN, WE WERE SO UNLUCKY NOT TO GET THROUGH…'

Before I joined my new teammates at the Ayr Scottish Eagles I decided to see if I could make a return to the Great Britain squad. To be fair, I did this for purely selfish reasons. I simply wanted to get in shape for the forthcoming season and to see if it had improved over the five years I had been out. It hadn't.

In August 1999 the GB Ice Hockey Board were given a six-figure grant from UK Sport to develop the game and the powers that be decided to take the team over to the Czech Republic to play some of the best teams the country could offer. The idea was to see if the team could learn from one of the world's mightiest hockey countries. As far as I was concerned it was a waste of time, effort and energy. Great Britain put together a team consisting of literally anyone and everyone as they tried to get enough numbers to go over. They flew in Wayne Cowley from North America who was in his mid-thirties because we couldn't get a goalie to come with us, which was completely unfair on him. Looking back, most of the team that competed didn't actually play in the Pool A qualifying tournament a couple of months later.

Taking us over in August was also a big mistake as we hadn't skated since the playoffs and the Czechs were in the throes of their season. We lost 6-1 against Znojmo, 3-0 against Dukla Jihlava, 5-0 against

Sparta Prague and got turned over by Ceske Budejowice 5-2 in our last game. Looking at those scores now it was actually ludicrous. It seemed to be organised as 'Let's go on tour here and see what happens.' In fact, those teams weren't the best in the country either – we were getting thrashed by some of the Czechs' second-string outfits. It was like a football club in Scotland going over to face Brazil. We really did waste money on that trip. The guys worked hard but there were loads of injuries because we hadn't skated in the off-season. Perhaps we should have gone to France or Italy – a country more on our 'level'.

Three months later, in November 1999, another squad was assembled to take part in the Pool A qualifying at Sheffield Arena. We were playing nations much better than our own but we gave as good as we got. I scored as we drew 2-2 with Ukraine and we then finished 0-0 against Latvia. In our final game against Kazakhstan we were one up through Stephen Cooper after fourteen minutes and were holding on for a victory that would have seen us through. With a few seconds to go, they pulled their keeper and first Rick Brebant went up the ice and passed when he should have shot, then I tried to beat out an icing call and hit the post. To add insult to injury, Andrei Raiskiy levelled the game just seconds later. Because the authorities had decided we had to play first to appease the television schedulers, it left the two remaining teams, Ukraine and Latvia, needing just a point each to go through and they duly obliged. Their game finished 0-0 with 16 shots on goal and that was it. Dina Bauba told me before the game that the result had been decided beforehand. It was almost certainly fixed.

A month later we took on Norway in Eindhoven in a fifth-place playoff with the winner going though to Pool A. We lost 2-1 but gave them an absolute battering all the way. Their netminder was immense as he kept out everything we threw at him. Yet again, we had been so unlucky not to get through and had to remain in Pool B. As a country we had stopped taking penalties against these teams and really started playing as a team but the result meant that the

UK Sport money was gone. They believe that if a sport is to receive funding it needs to be one of the top nations – that is, in Pool A. They would rather give money to an individual than a team.

I had to pull out of Olympic qualifying in February with a knee injury but was part of the squad that headed to Katowice in Poland in April 2000 for Pool A qualification. Again we were unlucky not to make it. Although we had an opening defeat to Estonia, 6-5, we tied with Slovenia 3-3 – when in reality we should have won – then beat the hosts 6-4. Poland had NHL top scorer Mariusz Czerkawski from the New York Islanders in their line-up but we managed to keep him at bay. There were nearly 8,500 fans shouting 'Polska' at once. It was great, like something out of a movie, and we played really well. I got a goal and two assists in that game. Two days later we beat Denmark 5-4 and then Kazakhstan 3-1. It set us up perfectly for the gold-medal match against Germany.

The Germans were already guaranteed a place in Pool A by virtue of being hosts in 2001, so they didn't need the points. However, they wanted to win the game just as much as we did. Early doors David Longstaff hit one of their players and put him right through the boards and all the players looked shocked. It rallied us and rocked them. We dominated half of the game until we got hit twice in eight minutes. The first went in off one of our defencemen and our net-minder Joe Watkins was screened on the second. We went on to lose 5-0. Again, we remained in Pool B.

Domestically the season didn't go according to plan. Despite bringing in eleven new players, the team didn't gel and Ayr finished a disappointing fifth in the Sekonda Superleague, made the semis of the playoffs, reached the quarter-finals of the Benson & Hedges Cup and came fifth in the Challenge Cup. Looking at the roster, there's no reason why we shouldn't have done better. The Centrum Arena was packed every match night, but we didn't score enough.

It's amazing how much money we must have spent that year! The club had nineteen houses, nineteen cars and nineteen families to look after and the excess baggage on flights was ridiculous. But that's the way the league was back then. Louis Dumont came in from Louisiana IceGators for just 14 games and he was the ECHL top scorer at the time, as well as having a whole host of experience in the WHL. We used him on the third line! Despite the controversial end to his career in this country, Scott Young was a character who gave everything. He always said what he thought and it was usually very coarse. Jan Mikel was another exciting player who came in from Italian side Milan Saima SG. Coach Jim Lynch knew what he was looking for but was very quiet and his man-management skills suffered. That was his nature but some of the players didn't accept it and it didn't help. Perhaps Jim didn't use me as well as he should, but when he left I led the league for scoring the year after. Whether it was a case of me moving to a new team and not doing well I'm not sure. I certainly didn't get enough goals, finishing with points, in the league, of 43 (8 goals, 35 assists), but the team didn't provide enough either. In my view some of the players didn't want to be there. Johnny Varga and Eric Murano had a fight after practice and that sullied the whole team. Shawn Byram was a good captain but liked to hold meetings behind Jim's back to decide on on-ice tactics for the next game that I felt didn't reflect well on his position and himself as a person. On the ice he led the team superbly and finished as the side's top scorer with 49 points.

Elsewhere, Superleague was wobbling. The teams were spending vast sums but attendances for the playoffs were poor. In fact, the number of fans heading to watch ice hockey had fallen by twelve per cent since the 1996/97 season. There were rumours that several clubs had broken the £500,000 salary cap and David Temme, chairman of ISL, surprised everyone by resigning. His predecessor, John Hall, had also stepped down at the end of the first season. David said that he believed the sport was being held back by an amateurish attitude. Both David and John encouraged the teams to spend big to attract the fans, but it simply didn't work. They were replaced by David Davies, who was originally Manchester Storm's managing director before he moved to Queens Park Rangers Football Club to be chief executive.

It was also sad to see my brother Paul retire after breaking his collarbone. He had been hit so many times by the puck and been smacked into the boards by opposing players that he had to call it a day. Paul was a great servant to Murrayfield and ice hockey in general, having played for Solihull, Peterborough, Fife, Edinburgh and Paisley. He was a real character, a renegade-type player who gave all he had, including several punches to opposing players, and the fans loved him. He is now working on the oil rigs on the north coast. He was a real loss to the game.

The following season Jim Lynch moved on and his assistant, Paul Heavey, took over as coach. Perhaps this was something that Paul wasn't looking for so early in his coaching career. In my view, he had come up from Cardiff the previous year with the idea of learning the ropes and helping out on a coaching team, but that didn't happen and he was thrown into the mixer.

It was sad to see Jim go. He was a good guy and someone I had known since Murrayfield but the team had to move on if we were to challenge once again. Paul came in with his own systems and ideas but despite me returning to the top of the team's scoring charts with 55 points, the roster never clicked. There was no reasoning why we didn't do as well as we should have that year as the squad was a real 'who's who' of the game in this country.

Household names such as Ed Courtenay, Teeder Wynne, Jonathan Weaver and Mike Harding made up the roster along with drafted tough guy Trevor Doyle. Trevor was a body builder who had been used to the American leagues and had found the Superleague not as 'tough' as back home. This meant he actually had to learn how to play, and really enjoyed it. You get this a lot with several enforcers who come over. If there's not enough 'action' over here, they will develop – or find, in some cases – their hockey skills! Apparently, Trevor is now a property developer and a multi-millionaire. He always said to us that he would be! Although it isn't an excuse, we did play that season with a lot of injuries – Dino Bauba only iced half a season and Mark Montanari was injured all the time.

During my career I have been very lucky with injuries, with my knee back at Sheffield being my only real problem. But I did receive two that could have been a lot more serious. At Bracknell in January 2001 I took a puck to the head from a Johan Silfwerplatz shot that severed my ear in half. I heard a whack and then a massive thud against the left hand side of my helmet and hit the deck with blood pouring everywhere. It turned out the force of the shot had pushed the helmet into my head and split my ear.

Now, trainers are supposed to be 'Joe Cool' when they come on the ice to reassure you that everything will be okay, but as I took my helmet off ours said, 'Holy fuck!' It wasn't the reassuring response I was looking for! Off the ice, Bracknell's doctor said he didn't want to stitch it because he thought I should go to a plastic surgeon but I thought to hell with it and thankfully he did a good job. Fourteen stitches to begin the collection.

A month later I went into a scramble with Trevor Doyle and Sheffield's Steve Carpenter and Trevor's stick came up and hit me – many thanks, teammate! It took a massive chunk out of my face. I was worried about how it would look but it's come out really well. Another six stitches. Thankfully I keep myself in shape so others don't come along, but these injuries are the hazards of the job.

In March we played a Sheffield team in the Challenge Cup that were later judged to be over the £450,000 salary cap by a rumoured thirty-seven per cent. The game was pretty tight until an error by referee and former teammate Moray Hanson turned the game on its head. It was 2-2 and he wiped out a perfectly good goal. Whether it had hit a skate or something, or there was a guy in the crease, it was a massive decision and they scored on the very next shift. We were furious. I know Moray said he had made a mistake afterwards and these things are there to be called but it was a real wounder. I know that Ed Courtenay was pushed into the crease and Sheffield claimed he had hit the goalie.

Over the past few years I have picked up the odd ten-minute misconduct penalty by shouting at refs because I just want my team to win so much. I have hit my stick against the boards a few times. Guys can call the ref anything under the sun on the ice and not get anything and then they can give a decision from 200 feet away. But Moray is one of the best refs around as he lets the game flow really well. People think he is our buddy, but he's hurt us a number of times too. He had said that I would make a good referee and perhaps that's something I should try. One thing is for sure: I would be ruthless.

Despite the disappointment of the Challenge Cup and our league form which saw us finish fifth (again) with a fifty per cent record, we headed into the playoffs with a head of steam beating Bracknell 4-1 and Manchester 6-2. Our semi was against London at the National Ice Centre in Nottingham and it was a really tough game but luck deserted us again. It was tied at 1-1 and London got on a two-on-one breakaway that resulted in an own goal from Silfwerplatz. They went on to win 4-3. That's hockey. Deflections as bad as that cannot be stopped, and sometimes they go the other way.

At the end of the season we again attempted to qualify for Pool A in Ljubljana, Slovenia, with Chris McSorley taking charge of Great Britain. The team was a blend of experience and youth and we got off to a flyer beating Estonia 6-2, then thrashing Croatia 10-1. Realistically, we had to beat Slovenia but drew 3-3, thanks mainly to an inspired Stevie Lyle who kept us in it in the first period. We could have easily been down 5-0. But we had a chance late on to take it when I came around the back of the net and Steve Thornton couldn't quite make it. Then we stuck twelve past China who faced 73 shots and finally went all-out against Kazakhstan to win 11-2.

That result meant that Slovenia needed to score at least twelve against relegated Estonia to go though. All the GB guys headed to the rink to watch the game but I didn't join them. From previous experience I just knew it wasn't going to happen for GB and that Slovenia would score the required amount. I just had a strong, strong feeling. Estonia were on their way out anyway and for me it didn't take a lot of working out that they wouldn't give it their all.

After they were only 2-0 down at the end of the first period I thought I was wrong so turned on the TV for the second. From then on I have to say that I have never seen such a shambolic team as Estonia. They never left their own end and they didn't have a care in the world. The game finished 16-0. It really left a sour taste in the mouth, especially with how the guys performed throughout the tournament. There were also strong rumours of Slovenian officials being seen outside the Estonian dressing rooms during the period breaks.

Whatever the case, I was disgusted and devastated for the lads. Although I have to say that I have played with a more talented roster on the national team, the chemistry among the guys was superb. Chris had taken on the job, unpaid, and was putting a team together while also coaching in Geneva. It really was the hardest job in the game.

Chris had us drilled really well and we were relaxed but focused all the way through the tournament. Off the ice there were some antics too. Chris was excellent in press conferences and was a journalist's dream with his quotes. Take these gems for instance: 'That's more rubber than the M1 sees on a busy day'; 'this result will make Slovenia's butts a little tighter going into tomorrow's game' – both after 73 shots were fired against China.

Michael Tasker and Paul Thompson also enjoyed themselves. During the competition we had a day off and the guys went for a few beers. Those two had a little more than others and before they got back decided to play a joke on Tommy Watkins. His hotel room was directly alongside the lift and the idea was that as soon as he opened the door they would go in and get him.

Sure enough, they headed up to his room, knocked on his door and ran in and then started beating him up. Unfortunately, it was the manager of one of the other teams! They had come out on the third floor instead of the fourth! There was an inquiry the next day and we all wound them up saying that the team had been fined and that they would both be sent home.

On the ice Chris had his systems and for some of the roster it was tough to play within them. He did let us play our own game, but we had to do it within his systems and for some it didn't quite work. I enjoyed the tournament, we played well and scored lots of goals but players were restricted at what they could do. The plan was to get it out of the defensive zone as soon as possible.

His system revolved around the team but didn't take into account if you had ten world-class players in it or not. It was completely new to some of the guys. Britain's 'old' systems were based on making things happen yourself. In my view, Chris' system did stifle flair players. I don't think that system is wrong or right, it's just my opinion. I have to say that the system he had in place didn't suit me personally, as one of the more creative players. But it worked for Chris and we did really well on the back of it. Once again we had gone close.

20

'IN REALITY, THERE WAS VERY LITTLE TO DISCUSS...'

Although the Ayr Scottish Eagles were a professional and seemingly profitable organisation (as much as you could be in Superleague back then) there were doubts going into the 2001/02 season that they would still be around come the end of the year. Yes, hockey in the area was doing really well – the team was growing in stature and fans were packing into the Centrum Arena – but the club was spending thousands on players, cars and houses and there were rumours that owner Bill Barr would be selling the club every soon.

At the same time, I had been considering my future and had an inkling that I wanted to try my hand at coaching. I was thirty-three at the time and it was something I always wanted to do. Most players want to stay in the sport as their playing career comes to an end and most want to coach. Yet the ones that make the grade are few and far between, and in this country opportunities are too infrequent.

I was wondering what step to take when during Mark Morrison's testimonial game in Fife I was approached by Mike Ward, one of the directors of a new club called Dundee Stars. He said he didn't know whether the Stars would be accepted into the British National League but wanted to sound out a few options with me. He asked whether I would be interested in taking the coach's role and I said I would certainly want to talk about it. In reality, there was very little to discuss. I would have been taking over a brand new team and had nothing to lose. There were no existing players there and it really enticed and excited me.

Weighing up the options, on the one side Dundee had a great rink, it wasn't far from home and it had a history of good hockey, but I also wanted to remain loyal to Ayr who had brought me up from Sheffield. I also had no intention of hanging up my skates just yet. So I went away to the World Championships with a number of things on my mind and I told Mike that I would make a choice when I got back.

On my return, one of the first things I did was to speak to Paul Heavey and the management at Ayr to see what was going on. The situation up there had put a doubt in my mind and Paul didn't really know what was happening as well. No players had been re-signed either and it looked like the Eagles management were keeping their cards close to their chests. I'd had a good year in Ayr and I wanted to continue to build on that but also wanted to keep my options open. For Ayr, I was the only Scot on the team so they wanted to keep hold of me, as they were the 'Scottish Eagles'. In the end they offered me a superb package, which would have meant becoming Paul's assistant. I would have been helping with everything on and off the ice and deciding what players to get in the roster. But I decided if I wanted to be a coach, it would have to be all or nothing and the Dundee offer was too much to resist. So I signed as a player and head coach in June 2001.

Apart from hockey schools, coaching was completely foreign to me. I had been around a large number of coaches to see how they worked but it was a real learning curve. The first thing that struck me was how much I needed to know. As a coach you are effectively in charge of someone's business – and that is frightening. A lot is riding on you and you can make the difference between that business succeeding or not.

With that in mind I could have been apprehensive but I can honestly say that the job never fazed me. I have always liked a challenge and although playing and coaching could have proved difficult I knew I would be fine. Besides, deep down I knew I would do well playing at that level. The hockey was a step down from the Superleague and this would let me concentrate on my coaching too. Don't get me wrong, I knew the BNL had some good teams in it, but overall I was confident I could play and coach.

Throughout those 'close season' weeks I didn't know what to expect and my first task was to create a team that the fans would love to watch and that could compete with the best teams like Coventry Blaze and Guildford Flames. The directors gave me a very good budget to recruit and after looking at the quality of the league through the rosters and how the other teams were recruiting, I knew where to go. It was a painstaking process and very time-intensive. Recruitment is the biggest part of coaching and if you do it well it can make a huge difference. I wanted a team with experience, as I didn't want to be coaching under-21 guys straightaway, and I was fortunate to land on my feet with several of my signings.

Having a budget was hard and looking back I was certainly a little naïve on what happened with it. I really looked after the money I had, paid the market value for players, but the number of outgoings opened my eyes. Houses, cars, flights, International Transfer Cards (ITCs), equipment, travel, national insurance, tax – there are a lot of things you do not see. People think that if 1,000 people come through your rink at a tenner a pop, that's £10,000 for the club. Once you deduct rent and other outgoings from that, the margins are really tight.

In my roster, I needed personalities and leaders on the ice so one of my first signings was to bring in Scott Young from the Eagles, who I have known throughout my career; he did well, and his team-mate Jan Mikel was next. Jan was a quiet man but a total professional who worked out every day, never drank and I knew that he wouldn't let me or the team down. Netminder Stephen Murphy was brought in from Fife to provide some safe goaltending, Martin Wiita was recruited from Sweden and I raided the Eagles again for Teeder Wynne and Patrick Lochi.

With these guys in place I knew I had the nucleus of a good team but that I had been lucky in attracting them too. In negotiating for them to come to the club I was asking them to step down a level from Superleague and also to take a cut in salary. In my favour, most Superleague clubs were reducing salaries. I also hoped that they would come with me because it was me, and because they saw what I was trying to do in Dundee. Some of the players I signed didn't get many offers and so came to see what Dundee was about. I sold the club to them and they agreed to sign. We were a hockey town and they trusted my judgement on it.

Perhaps in hindsight I was lucky with the quality of my signings but I was very upfront with them and told them my plans. In my mind I also wanted to bring the kids through and I gave chances to people who hadn't played at this level before. But that came back to bite me a little as some of the guys in Scotland wanted to be paid but didn't want to be professional. One guy I recruited at the beginning of the season came to pre-season training more than four stones overweight! In developing youth talent I also didn't want to entice players from the Fife and Edinburgh areas. I wanted them to be from the local area. Yet in that first season I needed my team to win in order to bring the crowds in so I couldn't blood the youngsters.

Thankfully, the directors of the club left me to my own devices to develop the roster and also let me get on with coaching. They trusted me implicitly and my mindset was to learn as quickly as possible and adapt. The directors showed immense respect for me and never influenced the team or what brand of hockey we should play. As a director you have to leave your coach alone or you might as well do it yourself. In fact, one of the terms I had in my contract was that I would be allowed to coach as I saw fit. I wanted to make sure I lived and died by my decisions and that they would support what I was trying to do. At our first game Charlie Ward, one of the directors, came and sat down in the dressing room to see what was going on. I couldn't let that happen so I had him removed!

Another part of my job was to be as high profile as I could. I tried to put myself out there as much as I could to generate some publicity in the press and help with marketing. The whole club did very well in that respect. The guys behind the scenes were selling the club and in those early days it helped the sponsorship levels, drove season tickets up and showed the professionalism of Dundee's new club.

But I did make a lot of mistakes in that first season, especially with my reaction to certain players. Within a few days I had to take measures to instil some discipline. I had to move one guy on because he was running up large alcohol bills in the hotel he was staying at while his house was being prepared. I just thought it wasn't on. I told the directors that I was not having a kid who I was giving a chance to drinking on my watch. It certainly woke some of the roster up as they realised I wasn't prepared to put up with that sort of behaviour.

Discipline-wise, I may have started off too strong. I wanted to be tough as well as professional and perhaps I overstepped it at first. In fairness, the whole team was really good with me. I love to win and if I see a player not trying hard it rankles me. Over the years I have learnt when to give it and when to hold back.

I didn't want the guys to think Dundee was being run like a holiday camp because we wouldn't have won anything. I'm from the 'old school' so I wanted the team to be disciplined and work hard. At first some guys would turn up to practice late so I had to put my foot down. The rules I had were: 'You're on time for buses', 'You arrive thirty minutes before practice', 'No drinking before games' and 'Look after your car'. These applied to all players. Even if you were earning less than others, I still wanted the same commitment and professionalism. Perhaps I wanted to win so badly that I was a little harsh sometimes, but I was always fair. I needed to stamp my authority early on as there were several strong personalities in the dressing room. It wasn't run like a concentration camp – in fact, compared to some, it was probably lackadaisical.

With the rules in place and a completed roster, the first practice session was one of the most nerve-racking things I have ever taken

part in. I learnt pretty quickly and had Colin Wilson and Roger Hunt as bench coaches to help me out. Our first game was ironically away at Ayr for an exhibition game on 24 August 2001. Before the match I had to give my first speech in the dressing room and again I was a little nervous. I got the guys ready for the game and told them what was required and perhaps in hindsight during that season I spoke a little too much! We lost 3-2 but drew the return fixture two days later 5-5. These games were a real eye-opener to me. I knew the team would be competitive but never expected to come close to beating a top Superleague team. Coming back on the bus from the first game I thought we had a roster that could bring home some silverware – we just had to kick on from there.

Playing and coaching was weird at first but I had set the team up pretty well in practice so that I didn't have to coach as much on the ice. I also developed my systems and tested others. There's only so many you can play anyway; once you know them it's a case of fine-tuning them and getting the right players into them.

We went into the season full of confidence and blew everyone away, going unbeaten in the league all the way through until November, when we lost 5-6 to Fife, who had also knocked us out of the Findus Cup earlier in the season. By the time December came along we had beaten Guildford 3-1 and 4-2, Peterborough 7-4 and 14-5, Fife 6-1, Paisley 13-1, 7-2 and 11-0, Hull 8-2 and 5-2, Basingstoke 4-2 and 6-5, Edinburgh 7-4, Milton Keynes Kings 5-2 and 6-2, Cardiff 9-0 and 11-2 and Coventry 6-3.

The early cup defeats had put some doubts in the league's other teams and I'm sure they thought that Dundee wasn't the team they thought. But we certainly showed them, losing only 4 games all through the year scoring an amazing 289 goals and conceding 101. Coventry was our nearest rival with nine defeats and two draws. To be quite frank, I think Dundee took the BNL to a different level that year.

With the competition between Coventry and ourselves, the league was attracting a lot of attention and thriving. The Superleague

was wobbling due to even more financial difficulties and a year later would be down to just five teams as, firstly, Manchester Storm were locked out of its MEN Arena for unpaid rent, folding later, and Ayr went the same way.

So I suppose it was the right time for the sport to have a strong BNL. Yet, for all the success we had, I have to wonder whether the league really wanted it. We had got into the BNL in front of the more established Dundee Tigers and that had created some bad blood in the town. But the league itself had teams like Guildford and Fife in it, who had been around for a while. They were spending big money and perhaps they didn't like a new team coming in and doing so well. With some of the refereeing decisions against us that year, I certainly had doubts about whether they wanted our success! One thing is for sure; we stormed the league and gave it a good shake-up.

If winning the league by a street ahead of Coventry, Fife, Basingstoke, Guildford, Hull, Edinburgh, Milton Keynes, Paisley, Peterborough, Slough and Cardiff – as well as taking the Caledonia Cup 8-5 on aggregate from Fife – was good, then taking the play-offs was even better – even though we probably gave a few of our fans heart attacks in the process. Both Coventry and ourselves had strolled into the playoffs, losing just one game between us. For the record, we beat Basingstoke 5-2 and 5-1, Guildford 3-2 and 3-0 and Milton Keynes 3-0 and 5-0 in the group stages and hammered Fife 10-3 on aggregate in the semis. Coventry had overcome Guildford 10-4 in the semis.

The first playoff game was in Coventry and we dominated from start to finish leading 7-3 with two minutes to go. As the clock ticked down, Stephen Cooper threw the puck to the centre of goal and it went in off someone's skate. At 7-3 I thought it was all over, but 7-4 gave them a real chance in the return leg.

And so it proved. A day later Coventry came to our rink and threw everything at us. Paul Thompson had them all fired up and, to be honest, we probably got away with it. There was no score after the first period, and then they hit us with goals from Stephen Cooper

and Claude Dumas to bring themselves within one on aggregate. Then we got a huge slice of luck.

The game was a corker, but very tense. Midway through the second period, I took hold of the puck and attempted to pass it cross ice. Luckily for us, it hit Cooper's skate and flew in, restoring our two-goal lead. At that point I thought the tie was over, but they scored again in the third with eight minutes to go to keep it really tight. In the last few minutes they tried everything but couldn't get past our netminder Stephen Murphy and, as the final hooter sounded, we went bananas.

Looking back I wouldn't take anything away from my team but I suppose we just hung in there. Thommo's team was superb that season and although he was down afterwards, I knew he would be a winner very soon. We had gone into the season with no expectations, but my experience told me that I was in for a good year. We never set ourselves any targets, but we knew we had to do well, especially with the budget the directors had secured for me. I cannot take all the credit – it was the players who did the business for me. Teeder Wynne came out with 94 points in 44 games (44 goals, 50 assists), Jan Mikel, who was excellent all season, got 85, Scott Young bagged 84 with 167 penalty minutes and Martin Wiita – probably the best player in the team – scored 66. Even when we were under pressure, Stephen Murphy was excellent between the pipes. He finished with a save percentage of 91 and had 6 assists!

After the playoff win, both sets of teams headed upstairs to have a few beers together. But the next day I was holding a hockey school so I left early without even having a drink, just chatting to a few of the guys and an inconsolable Thommo. It was weird leaving the rink early, but I didn't want to be there to get a pat on the back or anything, that isn't my style. I always think you get more out of a win like this if you enjoy it and stay off the beer. What's the point in getting hammered to a point that you can't remember it the next day and feel terrible? There's plenty of time for that. I've always preferred to go home and walk the dog!

For me, the year was amazing and beyond my wildest dreams. I finished the season with 104 points, with 25 goals, 79 assists and 18 penalty minutes. It also was a milestone as I became the first player in Britain to score 1,000 goals. In following years, Rick Brebant and Doug McEwen would achieve the same feat. It came against Hull as part of a hat-trick in Dundee on 19 January 2002. I remember intercepting the puck at 16.20, going down the other end and scoring a shortie past Stephen Foster. To be honest, at the time I never thought anything of it because we were struggling against a really good Hull team. In the end we won 5-3. It wasn't until afterwards that I realised I was the first person to do it with Rick being the second a year later. I knew it was on going into the game but also that I had plenty of time during the year to achieve the feat.

The trophies were an unexpected part of the season and I have to say that it was one of my best in British hockey. The team was fantastic – I was coaching friends and it was superb. I did make mistakes; perhaps I was a little too keen sometimes, but I wanted to win sometimes more than the players. I also took the Coach and Player of the Year awards.

The only downside, apart from not making the Findus Cup final was Scott Kirton leaving on deadline day. I gave the guys four days off after a win to recharge their batteries. It was around Christmas time and our next fixture was against a not particularly strong team so I felt we could get away with it. I felt it was important that we all took time away from the rink to relax and get ready for the final push.

On the day we got back I could smell drink in the dressing room. In fact, the place reeked of it. I thought that wasn't on, because they'd had all week to do it. Scott had a reputation for enjoying himself so I told him it wasn't on. Some guys in the dressing room were easily influenced and logic told me that he was the instigator. I told him that it was unprofessional and it wasn't right. I said that the days off were to relax, not to turn up to practice stinking of drink.

He said that he wouldn't do it again and apologised, but a week later he quit and went back to the ECHL with Pee-Dee Pride. I thought it was very unclassy of him to do that. He had been told and apparently he didn't like it. I was never that hard on the guys but obviously he didn't like it. I told them all that we were portraying an image of professionalism to the public, media and sponsors and that's how it was going to be run.

It was a shame because Scott was a good player who had been drafted by Chicago Blackhawks in 1991. Up until then he had posted 32 points in 22 games and had done a good job for us. Perhaps Scott tried to say 'I'll show them', but he cashed his cheque, went home and left us with a hole in the roster. It seemed preplanned. People had actually warned me not to take him in the first place but I had given him a chance. It showed my inexperience, to be honest.

At the end of the season I went across to Szeskesfehervar and Dunaujvaros in Hungary with Great Britain for what was my last year with the team. I hadn't announced my decision to quit, but some of the guys in the dressing room knew. Perhaps I was out of my mind going over there. I had finished the season top of the scoring charts, but I didn't have a great tournament. The season had caught up with me.

I was set in my ways and I wanted to help my country out, but I never played well at all. I was flat and should have had a break even though I finished as the team's top scorer. Again the team didn't click, despite being full of experienced players, and we did not score enough. Demark finished top and were promoted with Hungary second, Norway third, ourselves in fourth, Romania fifth and China in sixth. Injuries to David Longstaff, Jonathan Weaver and Steve Thornton didn't help but we got off to a bad start, losing 3-6 to Denmark, then 1-4 to Hungary. It was always going to be uphill from there but we beat Romania 5-2 and then China 8-3 before going down 2-1 in the bronze medal playoff to Norway.

At the end I announced my decision to quit the GB team for the second time. I had seen what was going on and in my view nothing was changing; we were still relying on dual nationals to carry the team. I didn't think it was going anywhere and I wanted to give the kids a chance. I did enjoy my time with GB but being away for two weeks didn't appeal to me anymore.

What did put me off was seeing Lobby (David Longstaff) in hospital. He suffered a blood clot in his leg and when I went to visit him, he looked like he was in a psychiatric ward – it was that bad. He got some form of deep vein thrombosis and I really felt for him. Being stuck in a foreign hospital, a real dive, for ten days must have been hell on earth for him. He was unable for move. In the end, when we were going home I couldn't say goodbye to him, I felt so bad. It was the icing on the cake for me and I realised that I had made the right decision.

21

'IT WAS A HARD SITUATION
TO BE IN...'

One thing about being at the top is that you are always up there to be knocked off. After the amazing double-winning 2001/02 season, Dundee had high hopes that they could continue to dominate the BNL. Once again I was given a good budget to put a roster together and I had to make sure the balance was right, especially with Coventry Blaze recruiting well over the summer.

I kept a strong spine of the championship winning team with Martin Wiita, Jan Mikel, Patrick Lochi and Teeder Wynne returning, but for some reason my other roster choices did not click with these players and we endured a bumpy ride all year. Expectations were high but the chemistry in the team was not as good as it had been before. On paper we were excellent; free-scoring and defensively sound, but what I hadn't counted on was the number of differing personalities in the dressing room.

In reality, it was my own fault. I was looking for someone to bring leadership to the side and I thought that Ken Priestlay, my former teammate from Sheffield, would be ideal. To be fair, it was a big mistake. He was a friend of mine and I was convinced he could do a job so I coaxed him out of retirement. In Sheffield they called him the Messiah, which was ridiculous considering there were a lot of good players at the club, but he certainly had an impact on Dundee – not for all the right reasons. I think Kenny expected an easier time as the league was at lower level than Superleague, Either way, he didn't do what I wanted of him.

Teeder was another player who surprised me in the early days. When I was putting the team together, he sent me an email asking why he wasn't the first guy I signed. He was really upset. I had signed Jan Mikel first as captain and Teeder was not impressed. I told him he was more than welcome to find another club and perhaps I should have made changes straightaway knowing his attitude.

Both players did well on the ice, scoring in abundance, but when you have a team you need to get away from cliques and that's what happened that year and I'm convinced Ken and Teeder were part of that. I was travelling up to Dundee on a three-hour round trip for practice so I never saw the guys that much and several close-knit groups developed. A lot of guys followed others, some blindly, during that season. I thought Ken and Teeder would have been more like leaders but they followed other people off the ice. In the end I have to say that I didn't trust a lot of the guys. Some of them just didn't respond to what I wanted, nor to being told what to do. I also had some players telling others the opposite of what I was telling them. I did feel that some of the team was working against me.

Some of my other roster decisions didn't work out either. Scott Young had gone to Hull Thunder during the off-season and I wanted to bring him back because he is the type of dependable guy who gives all for the shirt. I managed to entice him back for only nine games before he left to go back to Hull. We just couldn't meet his demands. I also got Mike Harding in from liquidated Ayr but he picked up a sore knee playing for us that turned out to be something he had brought with him and not told our medical staff about.

Dan Ratushny, who had played for HPK Hameenlinna during the 2001/02 season, came in midway through the campaign to help out because we had injuries. Perhaps I 'panic bought' because I wanted to win the league again. Dan was a good player, but he fell out with Ken early on for a ridiculous reason. It turned out that there was a rift between them because Ken had failed to pass to him during a game. As a coach it is difficult to resolve those situations without being frank to them. I told them what I thought but the rift was never healed. I also had nine imports at one point and it meant not playing guys who were friends with others. It was a hard situation to be in.

Dan didn't help matters when he decided to give up a weekend with the team to go away with his girlfriend. He said he couldn't make it because he was injured. I asked him who he was going to see because we had our own physio, and I said if he was having a weekend off he would have to get some treatment. I had arranged this, yet he cancelled the appointment saying he was going away with his girlfriend. He claimed that all he needed was a whirlpool because he knew his own body. I went off on one on the phone to him and told him in no uncertain terms that I was really unimpressed. I was annoyed that other guys were doing their bit and he was having a weekend off. But in the end it was my own fault; I had recruited these guys, so had to live and die by how they performed and what they did.

Looking back, there are various reasons why the team didn't gel. On paper, we were a class outfit. Perhaps there were just too many personalities at the club and they didn't respond to the hype we had created the year before. It wasn't all bad though; I was really impressed with Martin Wiita, who proved to be one of the most reliable players at the club. He showed up, played well and did his own thing, giving everything for me and the team. He was very quiet and I wish I'd had a load of players like him. Johan Boman, who came in from Bjorkloven IF, also did well.

My mind may have been on other things after an incident in Coventry during February 2003 left me facing a court case. On the fifteenth we faced a Blaze team who were really flying and had just wrapped up the league title. The game itself was fairly subdued, because effectively there was nothing to play for, but with the rivalry between us, both teams went for it. During the second period, we were on our way to a domineering 5-0 win when I was involved in an altercation with Blaze's Gareth Owen.

Owen had been in the penalty box for a minor and as he came out he checked, then dispossessed me leaving me on the deck. He then went 'one on one' with the keeper and nearly scored. I wasn't impressed so had a chat with him and we ended up fighting. We both got minors for the scrap and were sent to the penalty box. Once sat down, I saw something out of the corner of my eye – something silver – and I pushed it away. I was really startled because it was unexpected. I had my back to the object and when I glanced around to see what it was, it was a guy who later turned out to be Joe Featherstone. I was really surprised that someone had come into the box so I told him to 'get the hell out of here', or words to that effect.

Just think, you're in the penalty box, concentrating on the game and suddenly someone or something is beside you. It should be a vacated area so you never expect something to be in there. In fact, it is part of the playing surface. I saw something in the corner of my eye and I just pushed it out of the way. I never grabbed it, or punched it.

Then I didn't think anything of it, finished my penalty and skated out the rest of the game. Back in the dressing room there was a knock on the door and two policemen were stood outside waiting to speak to me. They asked me to accompany them to the station as the guy had made a complaint of assault against me. He claimed I had punched him in the face and, as a result, broke his glasses.

Down at the station I was dumbfounded about what had happened and thought it would all be over in a few minutes once they had checked the video of the incident. But I was placed in a cell for around four hours, hearing real criminals come in and out of the place. I really couldn't get my head around what had happened and it was pretty weird being in there. I gave a statement and Featherstone gave his version of events, with his wife, who had been in the stands, claiming she had seen and heard everything. Not bad considering how far their seats were from the box.

In the days that passed I learned he made a thing of complaining and that he was well known down the station. When I mentioned his name to some of Coventry's directors, they tutted and rolled their eyes. They all knew him! In fact, I still believe to this day that the police treated me apologetically because they thought it was ridiculous too. Nothing they said or did was illegal – someone had made a complaint and they had to follow it through, but I could just tell they thought the whole thing was ridiculous. Featherstone had also been in trouble with Coventry City Football Club and, apparently, had approached the penalty box a couple of weeks prior to the game to 'speak' to another player. He had also been warned not to do it again by the rink management.

Anyway, the police inspector viewed the tape and, no doubt wary of a complaint against them from Featherstone, charged me with assault. I thought that they copped out, pardon the pun. I believe they were concerned about repercussions and wanted to let the thing take its course. I was gobsmacked. Someone had left their seat to come down to abuse me – showing intent – and I was the one in the dock. What if he'd have done that to Paxton Schulte or some other hard nut?

In the next five months until the case came up I was really worried and wondered what the outcome would be. I had to fly from Edinburgh to Coventry on a number of occasions, which was a real pain, firstly to be charged, then to have my fingerprints and DNA taken and to plead not guilty. Yes, it was that stupid. I certainly clocked up the air miles.

When the case came up in August, Featherstone had been busy, going to hospital claiming he had bleeding behind the eye, headaches and had had difficulty sleeping. Later, it would turn out that the bleeding had been caused by a diabetic illness he had, but he claimed I had caused it. Looking back, I don't even remember catching him with the push, let alone causing damage.

In court, he pulled out a pair of glasses that had lenses missing and were twisted but we had a witness who handed them back to him at the match itself who said, under oath, that they weren't the same ones – or the damage wasn't as bad as the ones he produced. My lawyer, a guy called Chris Pendleton who was recommended to me, also proved that Featherstone had a criminal record – something that he had denied earlier.

During the case Featherstone decided that he wanted to leave the court because he was 'ill' and had to go home. He left the court to phone the doctor. It was like a comedy show. The judge was excellent to keep it going as I think she realised Joe was in a mess and was looking for a way out. In the end the judge watched the video, heard the evidence and found me not guilty. She said she was 'satisfied that there was neither intent nor recklessness in the act of Mr Hand who reacted to something that took him my surprise'. I was very relieved and have to admit that I had several tears in my eyes at that point. Leaving the courtroom Featherstone's lawyer approached me and wished me all the best for the forthcoming season. I think, deep down, he knew it had been ridiculous as well.

As for Joe, he was banned from all matches, both Blaze and Junior at the SkyDome and I later learned was also barred from all Coventry City FC fixtures and from teaching kids football. Coventry Blaze also changed their penalty box procedures by removing the simple barriers that kept people out and actually installing proper penalty boxes.

It was the end of a very stressful five months. Thankfully, I had the backing of my family who were really strong behind me, but it must have been a hard time for them as well. These guys do not realise the pressure that occurs to the supposed protagonist when these incidents occur. I had viewed the tape many times before the case and I still believe, as I did then, that it was absolutely stupid that it went to court. If I had been found guilty I would have had a criminal record, wouldn't have got the MBE and who knows where I would have ended up. If he had won the case, he probably would have come at me in the civil courts and I have no doubt he would have won. I was glad the judge took her time and let it run its course and found me not guilty. I was furious it had gone that far because I did not want some guy like that ruining the reputation I had built up for a number of years by treating people well.

It may sound like the season was a disaster; far from it. For any other club it would have been a good year. We finished second in the league, losing eight games behind Coventry. We also made the semis of the Findus Cup and playoffs, but failed to convert our chances. I missed the playoffs because I was suspended by the club, with Ken taking over, and later in the month I left the club by mutual consent. It was a sad way to end the year but one that I drew a lot of experience from. I finished the league season with 80 points (22 goals and 58 assists), with an additional 22 in the cup. I was also named on the BIHWA All-Star First Team (BNL).

During the summer I was approached by Neil Black, who was looking to put a team in at Braehead in Glasgow for the new Elite League, which would include a few other teams such as Coventry Blaze and Sheffield Steelers. I met with Neil in a hotel in Glasgow and he talked about what his plans were. But the decision to establish the team was delayed for some reason so I decided to take up the player/coach position at Edinburgh Capitals. I had been speaking to Scott Neil about the club during the close season and the opportunity was too good to miss. It was a job I had always wanted and meant I could stay at home with my family.

At the time, staying in the British National League (BNL) seemed a safe option, but the league was in a battle with the new Elite Ice Hockey League (EIHL) over control of the sport. It was a real mess that split hockey and something that no doubt drove fans away. In fact we are still recovering from it. Superleague had come through a turbulent time to start its seventh year with seven teams but, after the end of the 2002/03 season, had collapsed owing £22,567 to the taxman, £510,044 to unsecured creditors and £28,551 to Ice Hockey UK (IHUK). Manchester Storm and Ayr Scottish Eagles had also gone bust leaving the league with five teams. London Knights were homeless after Anschutz sold their London Arena and Belfast were teetering on the brink, owing something like £1 million.

The directors of the top Superleague teams decided to launch an 'Elite League' on the premise of developing British talent as well as sustaining professional hockey on a level playing field. But the sport's governing body, IHUK wanted a joint league. In the end this was unachievable as personalities at boardroom level in both the BNL and the EIHL couldn't agree on the best way forward.

When the EIHL applied to be affiliated with IHUK they were turned down because of funding and its financial structure, and the sport descended into farce. The EIHL said it would go ahead anyway – effectively going 'rogue', without affiliation – and the BNL started sounding off about it being the top league.

The Elite then affiliated itself with the English and Scottish Ice Hockey Associations and linked with the English Premier League to bridge the gap between the British players and their organisation. They also set up a party to discuss amalgamation with the BNL in the future. Cue the BNL! In a press statement they said that the EIHL was 'rogue' and that it had serious implications for the sport. It then announced that the BNL would go ahead not to cause any further delays and potential harm.

The farce ended with the EIHL being accredited by IHUK and announcing eight founding members – Basingstoke Bison, Belfast Giants, Cardiff Devils, Coventry Blaze, London Racers, Manchester Phoenix, Nottingham Panthers and Sheffield Steelers. The BNL went with Bracknell Bees, Dundee Stars, Edinburgh Capitals, Fife Flyers, Guildford Flames, Hull Thunder and Newcastle Vipers. It was a sad time to be involved in hockey but at least we had two leagues to play in. Me? I was looking towards the future back at my home rink.

22

'MADE IT THE PERFECT YEAR...'

I'm sure if you asked most players about their ultimate coaching job, most would choose taking charge of their home-town club. Yes, the top teams may come knocking sometime and we all dream of working with them, but deep down, the thought of taking your home-town club to the top and nurturing young talent has to be too good to resist.

The summer had been one of the most traumatic of my life; especially sitting and watching the Stars finish their playoff programme while suspended and the assault court case. There was uncertainty in my life but on the ice I never expected to be out of a job come the new season. In Britain, if you can play to a decent level then you should always be able to find some employment. High on my agenda was to keep in coaching, and while I was flattered by interest over the summer from the Steelers and Blaze, I would have just been a player there.

With import hockey the norm these days, the fact that clubs still want me as a player is really flattering. It shows that at my age I can still do a job on the ice. I have been offered a few playing positions in the last few years and I have certainly been interested because one thing I have learnt, especially at Dundee and latterly at Edinburgh, is that being a player/coach is very tiring. Sometimes I would have loved to have gone out onto the ice as just a player and not had to worry about twenty other guys and what they were up to on the ice. Also in my mind was the fact I wanted to keep my feet on the ground after what happened in Dundee and not take any chances – and that meant not stepping up to the Elite League as a coach, although the only 'offer' that came was Glasgow. So Edinburgh was the only logical choice for me. I knew the people there, had worked with Scott before and it was the right thing to do. I knew it was going to be tough though, as historically the Caps have struggled, but that season we had a great year and with a little bit more luck with injuries I'm sure we could have won the league.

During the close season, Scott secured sponsorship to bring me to Edinburgh and started to put the team together even though he didn't know who was going to be in place as coach. He recruited well and made sure he had a good spine of the previous year's squad for the new season. He had lost defenceman Paddy Ward and John Downes to rivals Dundee, who had done a great job the year before, but re-signed Adrian Saul, Steven Kaye, Martin Cingel, Jan Krajicek, Mike Clarke, Steven Lynch, Iain Robertson and Ladislav Kudrna before I came in. My first signing was Miroslav Droppa, who was superb all year.

Scott did a great job recruiting in those days and has done an even better one keeping Edinburgh where they are today. While other teams have gone bust, he has kept the Capitals going for seven years, on a smaller budget and fanbase than most others. Perhaps he takes on a little too much in terms of the running of the club, but this shows how dedicated he is to its survival. One thing about Scott is that he honours his deals. Never has a player joined or left Edinburgh without what they were promised – which is amazing as he is tight as a duck's arse! If you want anything from him you have to ask, and usually more than once.

In the locker room, Edinburgh had a great bunch of guys who played as a team and looking back were probably the best person-alities I have worked with. It was also a very disciplined team with no player finishing the season with more than an astonishing 42 penalty minutes. Even now I try to sign players who are tough but very disciplined. I hate indiscipline when I am playing and coaching – especially the guys who take ridiculous penalties at stupid times that hurt the team. My ideal player should have toughness and know when to use it, someone like Paul Ferone who iced for Newcastle Vipers in 2005.

He's tough, everyone knows that, but he doesn't just play the role, he is a good hockey player. Players have a lot of respect for these guys – they are tough, but they don't have to prove it all the time. I like guys who know when the right time is to do something, but not the ones that take a rash penalty and put the team under pressure. You never see Paul suspended or in the penalty box. I have never had anyone has tough as him in any of my rosters, but he's the sort of guy I want in my team.

One thing I had learnt from Dundee and my experience as a player was that I couldn't hammer the guys all the time. I couldn't have a go at someone because they had screwed up, regardless of how many times you had told them, if they simply didn't have the talent to get it right. This isn't the NHL after all. We are in Britain because that is the level we are playing at.

For example, if you want a player to 'quarterback the powerplay', there's only so many guys who can do that in this country. Perhaps in the past I was a little too harsh on some players that couldn't do everything I had asked of them. But that's the learning curve I was going through. I took the stance that as long as the guys gave me an honest effort, listened and did what wass asked of them and they were okay in the dressing room, then that was fine with me. Besides, if you have to tell a player every time they do something wrong, then perhaps you shouldn't have signed them in the first place!

While at the Manchester Phoenix, Rick Brebant said that being an effective player/coach in any league is tough and I would certainly agree with that. Sometimes when you give a player a hard time, next time they walk in the dressing room they will ignore you, and that could last for a few weeks! As a coach you can try and sort that situation out, but if you have to play with them as well, it makes it twice as hard. Therefore, you cannot go straight into the dressing room and stamp your feet – you have to be understanding and try to give and take a little more. I have never changed my coaching style since I started out, but I am a bit more understanding with the level of player I work with these days. At Dundee the guys were getting paid really well, so I expected top performances from them, but at Edinburgh we were not paying top dollar, so I could only ask so much.

Some guys, especially the Brits, are only earning buttons so it is difficult to be pissed off with them if they make a mistake. But if your franchise player is earning top whack and not performing, then that is a different story. You have to do something to protect the club, which is your role as coach. You wouldn't be doing your job if you let players waltz in and rip the club off. In my view, player's wages have dropped so drastically these days that we are being unfair on some of our younger players in the demands we place on them. We expect them to make practice and give all at games but they get little in return.

Perhaps the reason younger Brits are paid so little is because of our reliance on imports. We are all waiting for the next British kid to be drafted, but we have not developed our home-grown talent that well – especially in terms of coaching, and this is why they are not rising to the top. There has been so much infighting between organisations and differing league 'heads' that it has damaged the British player – and that is not good development as far as I'm concerned. You can tell this is true because there is a lack of quality British players around these days. There are some good players such as Lobby and David Clarke, but it is tough for these guys to break through. In British hockey, unless imports are cut, there is no chance for the British guy and that will never move the game on.

Coaching British kids and players on low salaries has always been a challenge I like, because they can surprise you, but looking after an 'average' team compared to the rest of the league and playing is the most difficult job you can do. Organisations can do wonders with budgets and eke every last penny out of them, but if the team you are playing has spent double then it is twice as hard to compete, which I'm sure some fans do not realise. This is one reason I ignore the Internet! People don't realise that hockey isn't a level playing field in Britain at the moment and the World Wide Web gives them a chance to stir things up. So I just don't bother reading it! The comments could be from a fourteen-year-old kid who doesn't understand hockey or someone on the other side of the world. After twenty-five years of playing I don't have to listen to that sort of abuse – and frankly, I do not care!

Being a player/coach in that situation is harder than anyone can ever imagine. People have given me stick for not playing and coaching well, but when your team is not listening to what you require of them on the ice because they haven't the talent, then your game starts to become affected as well. In my second year at Edinburgh, I decided that being a player/coach in an average team was almost impossible to do well – and that was just two months into the season. Being a player/coach in a semi-professional team where you only see the guys a few hours a week is nigh on impossible. But you can break the mould. That 2003/04 roster was put together on a budget significantly less than some of the other BNL teams and we did remarkably well. Every player we signed stepped up to be counted and took us to third in the league behind Fife and Guildford. I really related to Kaye and Saul and our top line was revered throughout the league. We also finished 1-2-3 in the League scoring charts – myself with 21 goals, 63 assists for 84 points, Saul with 31+32 for 63 and Kaye just one behind with 29+33. They knew what to expect from me and we clicked. I never pushed them too hard because they gave their all on the ice and they all had a good year and contributed to the success of the team. That top line gave the team 209 points and with Droppa scoring 39 points from defence and Kudrna (Laddi) backing us up with a save percentage of 90.2, we were a force to be reckoned with.

Miroslav Droppa was a real find. We took him from the Slovak League's Liptovsky Mikulas HK 32 VA and he had an enormous shot. People often ask how I find these players and I have to admit that some of it is luck. Martin Cingel worked as an agent part-time and he helped Scott and myself grab some of these players. You also rely on contacts, friends and agents. Most of the recruitment in hockey is done through contacts and recommendations and then you do the research. It wasn't all down to Kaye and the others though, Jan Krajicek did everything we asked of him, as did Mike Clarke, Steven Lynch and Neil Hay.

It's fair to say that I didn't expect us to do as well as we did that year. Finishing third was excellent and we could have won it if Krajicek and Kudrna hadn't succumbed to injuries. We could always find a goal with the top line and we were consistent and disciplined. Our season didn't start too well, with 0 wins in 7 games through the Findus Cup and exhibitions, but once we found our feet we started to kick on. Our first win was 4-1 away at Newcastle in September and a month later we had beaten Dundee (5-3), Hull (4-3), Newcastle twice (5-2 and 3-2), Guildford (6-4) and Bracknell (3-1). During the season we beat Fife (something which the club hadn't done for a long time), Guildford and Bracknell away several times and these were clubs we weren't supposed to beat. We finished the season with 19 wins from 36 games. We also won the Capital Cup, beating Dundee 7-2 in the final, and were runners-up in the Caledonian Cup to Fife. Just as we had at the beginning of the season, we struggled towards the end, winning just 4 of our last 12, but that was largely down to injuries to key players. In the end, a 3-3 draw away to Newcastle saw us scrape into the semi-finals against Guildford but we lost 10-5 on aggregate.

During the season, while coaching and playing, I was approached by a number of clubs to play on a 'two-way' agreement, which would have involved icing for my club and playing selected games for theirs. Coventry and Sheffield offered me a deal, but I didn't feel it was right. In my view there was no way that any club would let a player of value play for another club and I thought the whole notion was ridiculous. If you were a coach, would you let your top player go and play for another club? What would happen if they got injured? What would the club and fans think? I could see that the idea was great for the younger kids contracted to Elite League clubs so they could get ice time, but some clubs took it too far in my opinion. Some grabbed young players from the English Premier League (EPL) to help them cover a few injuries and crow about junior development, but what it effectively did was show that some of the Elite League teams didn't have enough junior talent coming through. But some clubs managed to sign top imports from EPL teams and that just wasn't right. The idea of the EIHL was to create a level playing field and this made a mockery of it, to be honest. I was also sounded out about a return to the national team but I again declined.

The previous year had been mostly been one to forget but it is amazing how things can go up and down in hockey. Twelve months earlier I had been sat at home suspended from Dundee as they had a crack at the playoffs and now I had finished a season with my home-town club and took them from the doldrums of the BNL to nearly winning it. On the ice, the season would always be one I would remember but off it a curious letter early doors in the season would make it the perfect year.

I remember opening the official-looking letter and being dumb-founded at what I was reading. It was apparently from the Prime Minister's office and it was saying I had been nominated for an MBE. The next paragraph asked me if I wanted it. I instantly thought that someone was playing a joke on me but it insisted I was duty-bound not to tell anyone so I couldn't find out. The letter was printed on headed paper and looked official enough so I replied and waited to see if anything came out of it. A few months later, on 31 December, I got a call from the press saying my name was in the honours list and that I would be awarded the MBE. I was shocked and really surprised. I remember thinking they must have done their research about what I had done. To this day I do not know who nominated me, but I wish they would come forward and let me know.

I have never been one to talk about what I have achieved so I will always see the MBE as recognition for the services I have given to hockey over the past twenty years or so. I would like to think I have given a lot of people some good entertainment over the past quarter of a century and put a lot into the sport, such as playing for the national team and hosting hockey schools and that the MBE is recognition for this. But there are other people who have put in the same amount of time and more besides and I would hope I am not the only hockey person ever to receive it. I'm sure more are around the corner but it seems they don't give them out as much as they did when I got mine! Undoubtedly, the MBE also gave the sport a lot of press and that has to be a bonus too.

The actual presentation of the medal at Holyrood Palace in Edinburgh on 29 June 2005 was probably one of the most nerve-racking moments of my life. I took my mum Lorraine and her then fiancé (now husband) Eric, along with Melissa to the event and I was dressed in full highland regalia. To be fair, I never realised what a big event it was until I approached the palace and saw the amount of security on show. They pounced on me straightway because as part of my get-up I had a dagger – a skean-dhu (Sgian Dubh in Gaelic) – and obviously it posed a significant security risk!

Once inside they separate you into the category of the award you are receiving – knighthoods go off into a very plush room – and drill you on what the Queen will say. The most important bit of information is that once she shakes your hand, you have to 'do one'. With this in mind, I practised my bowing and got ready. In the presentation hall, they announce four people at a time and you have to stop every few yards before you get to receive your medal. I'm don't know why this is, but I'm sure it's so you don't get too excited before you get up there and you remember to bow.

Meeting the Queen was something else. I spoke to her for a few minutes and talked about the sport, she asked how the British team was getting on and also made comments on ice hockey being 'unusual'. I know it is cheesy to say but she was really nice. She made me feel quite comfortable as she spoke, so much so that any nerves I had just disappeared. It does seem like there are only you two in the room at the time and feels really personal. Then just as you are getting relaxed the handshake comes and you have to be on your way. Oh... you have to remember to walk backwards and bow before you leave – it's amazing how many people forgot to do that. It was a great honour and an amazing day for myself, the sport and the family. It isn't as grand as some people think though – you don't get a feed! You can have a drink of juice or something, but I suppose it makes sense not to have alcohol at the event. You can't have people pissed in front of Her Majesty...

At night, we all went out for a meal to celebrate and a few days later got some of Edinburgh's players and my friends to raise some money for a children's cancer charity. We actually raised a decent amount by showing people the medal and documentation that went with it. It was a great end to an excellent year.

23

'THE HARDEST JOB IN BRITISH ICE HOCKEY...'

During the off season I received a call from John Elliot, head of the Belfast Giants, asking me about my intentions for the following season. He mentioned that they may be looking at a structure change within the club, and wondered if I would be interested in taking on the coach's role. I have to say that I was interested straightaway. Belfast was a great, strong club with a fantastic arena and the fans had a great reputation. I also wanted to coach at the highest level, which was the Elite League.

I'm not saying the BNL wasn't fine, just like most coaches I wanted to test myself at the top and the Belfast job was certainly that. We chatted for a few weeks, with John coming over to Edinburgh, before a decision was made. I was in two minds at first because I had had such a good year in Edinburgh but something told me that the job was right. I have always relied on my instinct throughout my career and it was telling me to go for it, so after a chat with my family, and other players around the league, I decided it would be the right thing to do.

I like taking teams on which give you a full free rein and that was what John was proposing, which was exciting to me. I also wanted to keep playing so that had to be in the contract. John agreed and the deal was done.

The first thing that went through my head before and after I took the position was how much of a hassle it was going to be getting over there. I decided I wasn't going to move my family out to the province, because we were settled in Edinburgh, so I would have to travel over. Perhaps I underestimated how much travelling I would have to do, but I certainly got over my fear of flying that year. I was on and off flights four times a week and got to see my family for around two days before Melissa would be driving me up the road to catch another 5 a.m. flight.

It was certainly hard on them. Melissa is used to me disappearing off for days on end – it's part of the job – but I missed walking my dog Rudi and it was difficult to see my kids. Thankfully, John understood this and let me get home as often as I could. He was an excellent businessman and a good manager. Families and friends are far more important I think, and the sport, in the end, is just a game.

I can't say I caught the flying bug straightaway. I missed my plane on the first day I had to be over there and nearly missed the press conference that would announce my signing. It could have been a real disaster as Belfast had, knowingly or unknowingly, engineered a situation that had only seen existing coach Rob Stewart told his contract would not be renewed a couple of hours before I was to come in. More of that later.

I was at Edinburgh airport and stood in the Belfast line. But there were two flights travelling at 7 a.m. to Belfast – Easyjet and FlyBe – and as luck would have it I was in the wrong line. When I went to check in they said I wasn't on the flight and that I should try the other queue. I knew I'd cocked up. I didn't know two companies would fly to the same place at the same time. I got on a later flight and made the conference… just. It would have looked stupid if I hadn't have got there.

As I said, the situation surrounding my appointment and Rob's leaving wasn't great. Belfast had made their minds up that Rob was not going to have his contract renewed and as a company they had every right to make that decision. But he was only told a few hours before I arrived. Perhaps the owners could have handled it better and told him a lot sooner – I think anyone would have thought that.

Perhaps they thought the best way to do it was to give out some good news, then the bad, and then hit everyone with the good stuff once again. Who knows? But it overshadowed my signing in the end. They told Rob and then a few hours later, I came in. Belfast is and always has been a pretty professional team, but they could have handled the whole situation a lot better. In my view, if you release a coach you should give it a couple of weeks before you find another one. Of course, clubs have a right to do what they want to – and appoint who they want to – but it's a situation they could have avoided.

It soured my appointment somewhat and some of the press let the organisation know. Some of the media guys were anti-change because they didn't want the regime to restructure and I copped a lot of stick for taking the job. It was all a bit weird. Some wouldn't speak to me for months and the guy who wrote the match-day programme didn't contact me for around eight weeks either. It was a strange situation to be in and totally ridiculous! At the time I had to ask myself what I had got into and if it was the right thing. But I just wanted to do the job, so I sat back and waited for it to take its course. Any coach that went in to Belfast would have probably have got the same treatment. The situation was created by the Belfast directors and I was just in the middle I suppose. It wasn't my fault they decided not to renew Rob's contract. Things change. There's always somebody ready to take someone else's job, but the press didn't see that.

What people don't realise is the amount of pressure the whole Belfast organisation has to endure just to play hockey. Coaching the Giants is probably the hardest job in British ice hockey. Costs are amazing through travel and one of the things I had to do straight away was work with John to cut back. The club had a Creditor's Voluntary Agreement (CVA) against it from the year before so we had to be careful. The fans were keeping us afloat and owner Jon Gillespie, an excellent owner and a pure gentleman, was putting money in. The directors decided the club was going to be under a strict budget. This was fine for me, as long as they kept the budget how they said it was going to be, which they did throughout the year. Nothing changed on that score.

Apart from the financial pressure, you are also holding a beacon for hockey in the region as you are the only club. There is a great responsibility on you to do well. There's no doubt that Sheffield and Nottingham are big coaching positions, but they don't carry the same responsibility that Belfast does. The clubs in England are 'lucky' compared to the Giants. Nottingham, for instance, can go an hour up the road to some games and they can practise in their own rink. In Belfast, most of the time we were practising out of Dondonald, a council-run rink, and on and off planes. For any player that arrives in Belfast, it is tough for them. Perhaps people don't appreciate the lengths they have to go to, waiting in hotels, getting up at five in the morning and travelling for hours on end. Certainly, any success Belfast has is well deserved.

Because I wasn't living in Belfast it was tough. We would fly across for a double-header (two games in a weekend) then at the end of the game I would sometimes rush to another rink to get a lift with a linesman I knew who lived in Edinburgh. Other times I would get my head down in Gatwick, because it was pointless for me to stay in a hotel, then be up early to catch a flight home. Several times I was woken up by the cleaners. You couldn't get to sleep after a game in a hotel anyway. It was ridiculous, yes, and wasn't very comfortable either!

Our playing schedule that year was also a real nightmare – especially in the playoffs. It was the most ridiculous and scandalous schedule I have seen in British hockey. We played something like eight games in ten nights. The players wanted to play but they were concerned about the pressure on them. No other sport in the world would have had a schedule like that. It benefited the other teams and it was stupid. We had gone through a hard league schedule doing really well, then should have been able to take that into the playoffs. But to compete in those circumstances was ridiculous. No team with our schedule would have made it. Our goaltender was out on his feet. Players were mentally drained. It just wasn't fair and we should have been at the playoff finals that year. I'll come to that later.

While the travelling was hard for the whole club, I did have an apartment in Belfast city centre. Curt Bowen found some great houses for the guys and it really made a difference to morale. If guys are happy off the ice and the houses are great for them, it can make all the difference and makes a coach's job a lot easier. It was right in the city centre and next to a Japanese bar called Zen. I really got to know the couple who ran the place. They were from Northern Ireland and were great, as were all the people I met in the city.

I have to say that a few times in the season I was a bit lonely. I wouldn't have made it through if it weren't for Curt (off and on the ice) and George Awada who lived close by. Curt became a really good friend and someone I hope I will still be friends with outside hockey. I do like my own company, but sometimes I needed someone to talk to. I had a good time with those guys, but that was replicated in the whole club. One of the unsung heroes at Belfast is Richard Gowdy who runs the office – he does an amazing job. He's the one who keeps things ticking over. Between the four of us, John Elliot, Curt Bowen, myself and Richard, we ran it well.

It would be ridiculous to think that I wouldn't be worried about being in the city. You hear lots of stuff about the IRA, UDA and trouble in the streets, but Belfast is beautiful and the people are friendly. It has its problems, of course, and when they're in that area and under the political situation it has, they are often magnified. Directly across from my flat, Robert McCartney was murdered. I came back from the rink and kids were throwing stones at the police and I wondered what was going on.

Any player who joins the club has to adhere to a few rules. We tell the guys at the start not to get involved in any trouble in bars, not to talk about politics – because you are not qualified to speak about it – and to keep your nose clean. For five or six years no one has had any trouble. We have visited schools, supermarkets and done a lot of promotional work and everyone seems to like the club. It is a really fine place and I couldn't say enough about the people. It's a place I would recommend anyone to go to.

On joining the club I started to look at the roster. It was important that we got the right balance. Although it was never directly said, the club wanted a good team to show the league and Belfast what it was all about. I think this was also to counteract what had happened with Rob. Thankfully, the directors gave me free rein in terms of who I wanted to sign, but they did provide some input.

To be fair, I knew what I wanted and so that was not important. The directors left us alone and were excellent. In fact, I probably never heard from them all season apart from the odd email asking me how I was getting on. I really enjoyed this.

My first move was to re-sign defenceman Todd Kelman and draft in Martin Klempa from Slovakian side Poprad HC KP. These were very important additions to the roster as I wanted a strong D and netminder, effectively building from the back. Todd was drafted by the St Louis Blues (round six, #141 overall) in 1993 and had been at Belfast since 2000. I think he felt a little wary because of what had happened to Rob but he proved to be a cracking signing all year, although he was unlucky with injuries. I tried to get Jason Ruff back into the club but he decided to go to Kansas City Outlaws in the UHL instead.

Creating a roster was very hard that year because we wanted players to fit in our budget, and they had to be experienced. My former Edinburgh teammate, Martin Cingel, recommended Klempa and also Roman Gavalier and after some research they came in. Klempa was outstanding all season. He was a great shot stopper and Roman, who came in from the same team as Klempa, was great on the D. They were probably the most professional guys on the team.

Shane Johnson was next to be re-signed and then I started talking to the British guys – Mark Morrison, Graeme Walton, Chris McGimpsey, Marc Levers and Leigh Jamieson.

With a nucleus of a good team, I then looked to add some firepower to the forwards. This took a long time to happen and I seemed to spend most of the summer dealing with agents. I knew George Awada had been approached by Sheffield so I made him an offer and he took it. I knew with the training and travelling regime Belfast would have to put in that year that I needed someone who had gone through it. George had done this at Manchester so I knew he would be ideal. He had played for the Phoenix at the MEN, but was training at Deeside in Queensferry at all manner of stupid times in the morning. He went through a lot that season in a struggling team, and I knew he would be a leader, because he always has been.

In my roster I decided I needed experience because I didn't want players who had to be baby-sat. Todd, George and Jason Bowen (re-signed) were ideal and then Curt Bowen (re-signed) and Curtis Huppe (South Carolina Stingrays) came in. Fredrik Nasvall was one of the last to sign from Skelleftea AIK in Sweden.

Tough guy Mel Angelstad joined late from Portland Pirates and did a great job for us. A lot of people said that he would struggle playing-wise, but I liked what I heard and wanted to give him a try. He is probably the best tough guy I've seen. He doesn't care about fighting, so I had to calm him down a bit! In the end, he played some great games for us and was really solid in front of the net. People said he was a terrible player, but he wasn't there to score goals or set up the powerplay, just to make sure there was no rebounds and that no one was having a free go at our net. He only had around three fights that year but picked up 285 penalty minutes. It was important that we got in a tough guy. Belfast fans have a reputation that they do not want guys coming into their rink and beating up their own team. Mel certainly made sure this didn't happen.

My last import was a chap called Diarmuid Kelly who had played a handful of games for the Colorado Eagles in the CHL. He had seen that we were holding trials on the Internet and paid for himself to come over from Canada to give us a go. To make that effort showed me that he was committed and that he had a lot of character. He had great hands, and looked a lot older than his years – more like thirty-two than twenty-two! His skating let him down a little bit but he did a great job. I didn't have much money left for the eleventh and last import, so I made him an offer and said if you want to stay over here on that, go ahead. And he did. It was great publicity for the Giants to attract a player in that way.

Another thing that was strange, and sure, a bit lucky, was that all the guys that came in that year were single. It certainly kept the costs down.

Looking back, one thing I am really proud of is that I didn't change the team all season. At a time when players in the NHL were on strike, there were plenty being offered around and we were approached by several agents. It is true that some would have improved the team but what would have happened if the strike was called off and they went back to the NHL? Also what was the was the point in changing it anyway? We were doing really well and I think the players took great comfort from that and I gained a lot of respect from them.

I can't say I wasn't tempted though. I knew other players were coming into the league, but I believed my team was good enough. The NHL players were the best in the world, there's no denying that, but there was a cost involved. Unless they were coming in to enjoy themselves and to keep in shape, we had a CVA against us, so it was quite prohibitive to bring them in.

On the whole, the influx of NHLers was good for the league and created a lot of publicity. One thing is for sure: they certainly helped the teams they went into. Coventry benefited big time from Wade Belak of the Toronto Maple Leafs; no one can deny that and Thommo did a good job to sign him.

London, who didn't do as well, brought in Scott Nichol (Chicago Blackhawks) and Eric Cairns (New York Islanders), which made them one of the toughest teams to beat and probably the toughest ever to play in hockey. Nottingham brought in three players – Nick Boynton and Ian Moran (both from the Boston Bruins) and Steve McKenna (Pittsburgh Penguins) – but failed to live up to expectation once again. Their two D guys were superb players and were better than what they showed.

In Britain, we have always seemed to attract more of the tougher guys, rather than the skilful ones, but with all due respect, they couldn't go to Europe and play, so that's why they ended up here. In my view and I think most would agree, Belak couldn't have gone to Sweden or Finland and played his type of 'tough' game. Cairns couldn't have played in the Swiss A league, because of its different style. This doesn't mean that they are bad players. Even some of the other NHL players were struggling in those leagues. The European leagues are far more skilful but the hockey in this country, more North American style, suited their toughness. We always seem to bring over the tough players to improve our game and the number of rucks certainly went up.

I still think if the NHL had not been on strike we would have won the league that year. No disrespect to Coventry, who were superb through the season, but Belak boosted their team and gave it toughness, which they had lacked up until then. It made a big change and gave everyone in the Blaze a lift.

But my team seemed to bond better without having an influx of players and as a result my position was a lot easier. I had to speak to a few about how they were playing and get them to know my style and how I wanted them to play, but they were really professional and took on board everything I said. This meant I didn't have to do as much work with them as I thought I would.

There were a couple of guys who didn't like how I spoke to them. Or rather, not 'how' I chatted nor what I said, but 'why'. Perhaps they could have taken it better, but on the whole there were none of the problems that there had been at some of my previous clubs. When I spoke to players that were going through lean periods I just told them they needed to pick their game up, offered some advice on how to do it and they always responded. It wasn't a case of finger pointing.

For example, Curtis Huppe had come across as a goalscorer but early on hadn't put it in the net for something like 15 games. Curtis has to be confident to play well and he was feeling down, so I had a chat with him. It was never a conversation like, 'your job is on the line' or 'you have to start scoring' because that would put more pressure on him. Myself and Curt Bowen talked him round and then he went really hot and scored for games on end. Sometimes guys go on a lean spell, like we all do.

The way Belfast is set up, the whole team have to be completely professional and has to be 'into it', because of the travelling and the pressures on them. They couldn't get through it if they weren't and they would hate being there. The guys were fine with all this. We used to laugh about the flights because I had them flying into all the cheap airports like Bristol and bussing it from there to the games in England. They would get off the plane and wonder where the hell they were! As soon as you fly to Heathrow or Birmingham the price goes up, so it made sense.

The guys couldn't get their heads round it sometimes. I was in charge of the budget for flights so I booked them four or five months in advance to save as much as I could. Sometimes it wasn't perfect for the players, but they went with it and were excellent all year. Winning is important, I love to win, but the business had to come first. I made sure that we were within our means all the time.

When they joined the club, the imports knew what was coming and they knew they needed a professional attitude to get through the season. I wanted the whole team to adopt this mentality so it was the same for the British and Irish lads. They were great. They probably never had somebody like me before come in and make them responsible for what they did on and off the ice. I think it was refreshing to them and I'm sure they are better players for it now too. I asked questions of them on the ice and I was trying to teach them how to be professional. They weren't there to make up the numbers as they were a vital part of the team, so when they didn't play well, they were told like the rest of the imports. If they made mistakes or showed up late, they would be told like the rest of the roster.

Earlier in this book, I said that the British kids sometimes fail to take a 'professional attitude'. Belfast went against that because all of them were great. Marc Levers typified this and he has certainly benefited from it. Some players do not like coaches who tell them they are not playing well but he was one who really took it on board. Some didn't at first though. I had to have a chat with Leigh Jamieson who wasn't playing that well. Leigh forgets he is young sometimes and he screwed up so I told him. Afterwards he asked me for a meeting, and in there he told me he thought because I had told him off it was personal. That really pissed me off, and I told him.

Leigh is a good kid who has been professional for a while. Perhaps he thought he had made it, being at Milton Keynes and stepping up to the Giants, but being just shy of twenty he still has another ten years to go! It's not easy being professional; you still have to put the work in and perhaps I surprised him. I said in the meeting, 'If you have taken my advice and comments as personal, well that is the only way I know how to coach. If you do not like that, then perhaps you should be looking elsewhere.'

I have been professional all my life and I have never taken it personally when criticism comes. I have been told to pick my game up and dropped from first lines and you have to learn from it. I was trying to teach him how coaches think. I would hope that he has turned out a better player because of it.

On the ice, the season was a great one. It surprised me how well I did personally as a player, but as I was lining up alongside goalscorers, it was great to set them up and chip in with the odd goal too. The guys seemed to fit in with my style. I did have to alter how I played in some ways though. Nasvall was temperamental and Huppe struggled at first, so I had to adapt my playing and lines a little. Once again I finished top of the scoring charts with 75 points (20 goals, 55 assists). I made the BIHWA Elite League first team and got the Player of the Year Award. These days I am not interested in the points, but it was important for me to play well as I was on the ice all the time.

The Elite League was certainly at a higher level during that season than the year after. Whether that was because the teams were spending a little less or the fact that the NHL was back on and the players went back to the States, I don't know. Being back in the top flight meant I could make some comparisons and I have to say that Superleague was of higher calibre – just a little higher. Back then, teams were blowing thousands on three strong lines with imports. Now the third line tails off a little in terms of quality. That's what happens. The EIHL is good, but it isn't as good a level as Superleague. Superleague teams were spending half a million on a roster and now it's half that. It was important for me to make the step back up to the top flight and show I could compete on the ice and as a coach too. I'd like to think that I am pretty knowledge-able about the sport so I knew what I was letting myself in for, so I was always confident I could do a job.

That season, the team did the job I asked them to do. We got off to a cracking start in September, beating Sheffield 3-0 on the road and then drawing 3-3 with Coventry the day after in their rink. We were 3-1 up with around ten minutes to go, but they came back as we tired a little. Belfast never hosts any pre-season games as it is expen-sive to travel and get clubs over to the Odyssey arena, and it did show towards the end of those first few games.

A week later on 18 September we played our first game at home and lost 2-3 to Cardiff, but followed it up with a 5-0 win over London. Throughout the season we were very consistent and picked up wins against all the league's teams, home and away. In October we beat Coventry 2-0 at home and got off to a flyer in the National Cup, thrashing Guildford 5-1 and Edinburgh 8-1. One team we struggled against was Basingstoke who, no matter how many shots we put on them, always played amazingly well. At home in October we stuck 45 shots in but couldn't score, losing 2-0. Their netminder, Ronnie Vogel, was amazing that night. The day after, we lost to Coventry and struggled past the Racers at Lee Valley in overtime a week later.

The league was certainly competitive and all teams could take points off each other. Our Challenge Cup campaign seemed to have ended 5-0 in Cardiff, but we gave ourselves a shout in November by beating Nottingham at the National Ice Centre 2-1. I scored the winner from an acute angle on the powerplay and also got a ten-minute misconduct for smacking my stick against the boards! Sadly, we never made the semis.

The rest of November brought losses to Sheffield and Nottingham, draws with London and Basingstoke and wins against Cardiff, Dundee and London. December was a fixture-packed month and we beat London, Edinburgh, Hull, Fife and Nottingham, drew at Bracknell, and lost our only game in the National Cup, away at Fife 6-5 in overtime.

I made sure the guys didn't underestimate the BNL teams and it was secured on February 24 when Gavalier scored in overtime against Guildford to win 4-3. The BNL clubs surprised a few Elite teams and really took them on. On some nights, they played with the same imports as us because of injuries. The cup was a great idea, but we didn't get anything for winning it! Where was the shiny trophy? We won it, we won the competition and got nothing for it. It was a bit funny, eh? But that's ice hockey in this country.

Anyway, in January I wanted the team to kick on because we were in with a shout of the league title, being just a couple of points behind the Blaze. We beat Newcastle twice, Hull and Sheffield, took three points off Nottingham but lost to Basingstoke again after dominating the game. Coventry started to get further ahead, but I knew if we could keep close to them, we had two home games at the end of March where we could beat them and pick up the title.

February 2005 was probably the defining month of the campaign. We drew at Cardiff, lost and won to Basingstoke but beat Bracknell and Nottingham. On the 26th we battered Sheffield but Jaime Platt had a stormer in goal for them and they won 2-0.

Six days earlier we had lost 2-1 in Coventry after the referee disallowed a Curt Bowen equaliser. He was the only bloke in the rink who thought the net was off. I have seen it on video and there's no way it was. I gave him both barrels. Effectively, it was all over because we were a few points behind the Blaze, but we had to keep going. In March we beat Cardiff twice and Sheffield, but by the time Coventry came to our place, it was all over. In those 2 games 23 goals were scored: a 6-6 draw and an odd-goal loss.

It was hard to take, but I was really proud of my players. George

Awada finished the regular season with 60 points (34+26), Huppe posted 25+34, followed by Nasvall (25+28) as well as Curt Bowen with (24+28). The defence had chipped in really well and Klempa was outstanding, with a save percentage of nearly 93.

I couldn't fault them at all. We had finished runners-up, six points behind the Blaze with a record of 31 wins, 10 draws and 7 losses (two in overtime) for 71 points. We had scored 170 goals, 11 short of Coventry, but conceded the same amount as them, 104.

Klempa was certainly the netminder of the year but we did miss Kelman, who broke his foot with a shot and got a stick in the face. It was a bad one that cut him up. When you're as injured as that, it's tough to get your rhythm going again. Shane Johnson was in the wars too.

Going into the playoffs we were confident, because we had played well all season. Although we had fought hard for the league, going full-out for the last 20 games, we wanted to do well. Because of our league positioning we were drawn in Group B with Cardiff Devils and Sheffield Steelers, with Coventry, London and Nottingham in Group A. But as soon as the schedule was announced, I knew we were struggling. Apparently the problem was that teams could not get good dates for games, so we suffered.

We played Sheffield at their place on 17 March, losing 4-0 before waiting a week to take on Cardiff (1-2). Then we played Cardiff at home on the 26th (3-3), Sheffield away a day later (2-4), then the Steelers again at home on the 29th (5-5), before going to Cardiff on the following day (0-3) and retuning to Belfast to face Sheffield on the 31st (2-2). Two days later we lost 1-4 to Cardiff at our place.

Even thinking about that schedule leaves me angry. I'm not saying we could have won it, but we were never given a fair chance. During the playoffs, the players were tired and could, within rights, have refused to play. We were travelling back and forward and it wasn't even fun. It took me a full week to recover afterwards during which I hardly left my bed. We were probably breaking guys' contracts by making them play that much.

We took each game as it came and went for it, and went hard, but we never had anything left. The spark wasn't there. If we had been based in Britain then perhaps we would have had a fighting chance, but we couldn't even get flights that quick to get over to the games – it would have smashed the budget – so we had to rely on buses. When we played Sheffield on the 29th and the 31st, we had a game at Cardiff in between. The Steelers stayed in Belfast waiting for us to come back! It really did border on the farcical.

I was surprised we didn't get a win, because we didn't play badly at all, but we were very fatigued and not at all sharp. Klempa was out of it and some of the saves he had made throughout the season he couldn't make in the playoffs. It was the same with the whole team. We missed chances and didn't convert draws into wins.

The final in Nottingham passed me by because I was still pretty disappointed with the schedule, but Coventry won it, beating Nottingham 2-1 in overtime to take the Grand Slam. I was happy for Thommo.

Towards the end of the season I was undecided about what to do for the following year. I had started a job in Belfast, and wanted to take them further, but I would be lying if I said the travelling wasn't getting me down. In the meantime, Edinburgh had been accepted into the Elite League and I was really tempted to go back there.

I had been speaking to John Elliot about returning to the Giants, but nothing was finalised. As talks were ongoing, they lost the Rover deal and there was some doubts about what was happening. Jim Gillespie didn't want to keep putting money in and so there was a lot of uncertainty.

Perhaps this played on my mind, but with Edinburgh becoming an Elite League team and the club only being fifteen minutes from my house, I couldn't really turn it down. I had to be practical and I wanted to be near my family. It wasn't for money – I was making a lot less in Edinburgh than in Belfast, I can tell you!

One of my final acts on leaving the Giants was to recommend Ed Courtenay as their new head coach. I knew John was looking for someone to replace me and so I immediately suggested him. I am still friends with Eddy and have played with him at Sheffield and Ayr. He is a true 'stand-up' guy who I knew could take on the club and keep it going. Yes, it was his first coaching job, but I knew enough about him to know that he would be fine. It wasn't too much of a gamble for the club or Eddy and it certainly paid off the following year. Belfast had a core of players, but managing to bring in Theo Fleury was great for the team and the sport. And they were awesome all year, as was Eddy, who proved to be one of the club's top players.

It was a tough decision not to take on Belfast again. The uncertainty didn't help, and perhaps it swayed my decision a little. I told John it would be crazy not to give Edinburgh another shot. When I took the job on I explained to Scott Neil the budget meant it was going to be a tough year. It would also be a big step up for them. They were bottom of the BNL and now were expected to mix it among the big boys. Thank god I never underestimated how hard it would be.

24

'IT WAS PROBABLY THE TOUGHEST YEAR IN MY CAREER, THAT'S FOR SURE...'

When you are making the step up from a lower league to the highest, one of the first things you must consider is how much you're going to spend. Although you would like to compete with the bigger clubs, you have a duty to ensure the business survives the season and for the next ten or so years. Let's say you have to be realistic in what you want to achieve.

At Edinburgh, Scott gave me a significantly lower recruitment budget than the other Elite teams, but one that would ensure the club didn't owe thousands at the end of the season. As a coach, it is difficult to work with less money than the rest of your competitors, but I totally understood what Scott was trying to do. He understood the business and gave me what I needed to put a team together. Unfortunately, Scott is not as lucky as some of the other Elite teams, some of whom are paid to stay in the league. Even though Scott's Edinburgh Capitals were totally new to the top flight, he didn't receive a penny – it was all down to him to bring money in. A level playing field?

Looking at the roster you have to say there were no real superstars, only players who I expected to give a good account of themselves and the club. When I was putting it together I had to be aware of the money situation all the time and sign players that fitted into what we wanted. They had to be predominately single – because girlfriends and families cost more money to keep (!) – young, and reasonably priced. Straight away I was cutting my potential pool of players down. In effect, I wanted players that could give me 'good value' and could not attract the twenty-six, twenty-seven and twenty-eight-year-old experienced guys with families. Bargains, basically…

However, the roster did contain a mix of experienced players, college kids and amateur Brits, giving me something I felt I could work with. Neil McCann came in from German side Riessersee SC and was excellent all year. He was a real revelation for the club and someone who could have played for any other team in that league and done a cracking job. He added some bite to the top line and also had a degree in rocket science. One of my phrases in practice is, 'It's not rocket science guys' and you could see him throwing daggers at me! We lost him midway through the season because his dad was ill, but he did return for the playoffs.

We also recruited left-winger Travis Lisabeth from Mississippi Sea Wolves in the ECHL but he was only with us for 18 games. He came across to play and continue his schooling but it never suited him. He asked to be let out of his contract to go back home and I could see that his heart wasn't in it so accepted the situation. He's a better player than he showed at the Capitals. As soon as he got home he took up a position at Columbia Inferno in the ECHL. We also got in Mike Sandbeck and Mike Kiesman, who had both iced for the Reading Royals in the ECHL, to bolster the squad. They both proved to be excellent additions to the team.

Elsewhere, I went for a mixture of experience and youth with Martin Cingel and Dino Bauba returning, Jeff Marshall coming in from Dundee alongside Neil Stevenson-Moore from Princeton University and defenceman Jim Vickers from London Racers. Jim's experience meant he was ideal for captain. We also took on Jaroslav Prosvic, who had been released by Hull, to help us with an injury crisis later in the season. The young Brits did a job for us and developed throughout the year. Some of them still worked and so had to miss practice which made it very difficult to develop them further. But that's the way it was and they tried their best to give it their all.

Attitude was an issue in those early days as most of the team had not played in a fully or semi-professional league before. It was very difficult where to go with discipline because it was restrictive to bring other guys in. Sometimes we had guys missing practice and I couldn't really do anything about it. Yes I could have a word with them but I had to be practical about what I could really do. But on the whole the guys were good with me. Some of them liked to 'take the night off' on the ice sometimes because they were so used to losing. I did feel at times during the first few fixtures that they weren't that bothered when they lost and that was something I tried to change in the team. I wanted the guys to be as focused as possible, but it was tough considering where most of the team had come from.

Jeff Marshall was one player to show how naïve the team was at this level. Before a double-header he called me to say he had got a good deal on a flight, was off to Amsterdam for the weekend and he wouldn't be able to play. I was gobsmacked. Before the next game I pulled him in and asked him straight up if he was taking the piss. I asked him if he thought I was here to coach players that wanted to go off to Amsterdam for a weekend. I said, 'If you don't want to play here, I'd rather you just go and I will coach a younger lad who wants to be part of the team.'

Jeff turned round and said that 'this is how I thought it was...' He thought that was how the league and the club was, so I told him otherwise. Understandable from the level he came from, but unacceptable on my watch. He apologised and became a vital part of the rest of the season.

In the roster, only I had been recruited from the Elite League. The rest were players who had been part of the Caps team in the BNL and others from abroad. This meant we had a lack of experience straightaway and it showed in those first few months of the season when wins were few and far between. I always knew it was going to be tough to take a team from the bottom of the BNL to a decent position in the EIHL, but didn't think it would have been as tough as it was. We got off to an amazing start in the Challenge Cup, beating Sheffield at home 2-0, which was very encouraging for me and the fans, but lost 8-0 and 9-0 away at Nottingham and Newcastle to put us effectively out of the competition. In the final three group games we faired no better losing again to the Panthers and Vipers and losing 9-0, again, to Sheffield.

It was 22 October before we picked up our first league points – away at Basingstoke where we won 5-3. We then picked up a point in Coventry but had to wait until the end of November to record our first home win – against the Blaze. We took another point off them in our very next fixture. December was a nightmare as we didn't pick up a point, before 5 wins in 7 matches over January, including 3 wins against the Devils, took us ahead of Basingstoke to go seventh.

During this time I had to give our netminder Martin Kucera two weeks' notice. Martin is a pure confidence player who has to be supremely up for it to be on top. He came in from Slovak side Skalica HK 36 with great reviews and promise but at first practice I saw he was struggling a bit. I wasn't worried but after doing okay for us at the start, he started to let in goals that were pretty bad. When the team was playing hard he was killing us with six or seven conceded so we couldn't continue with the situation.

I called him into a meeting and gave him fourteen days' notice that he would be leaving unless he improved. It was hard to do as I like to stick to my players and give them all the support they need. To be fair he understood the situation and said he might not get a job next year if he kept letting goals in! He took it on board and was pretty solid for the rest of the season. He's certainly not a practice goalie though… he lets everything in!

Sometimes the team played really well and didn't get its rewards but other times you could see the difference between us and, say, Belfast. With a lower budget you were always going to see that difference. One thing I found was that when we had injuries we couldn't replace the players but other teams could. Some would have twelve imports on their books at any one time, when the rule was just eleven. But the regulations allowed for this and that made it difficult for the other clubs who couldn't afford to bring guys in to compete.

At the Caps we had to make do and put players out there who shouldn't have been competing at that level. Sometimes we played with just two lines because we didn't have the players and got guys in from Lee Valley to make up the bench. Of course, this affected confidence in the camp and we struggled to beat teams.

When we had a full roster, we could beat the teams immediately above us and take the likes of Belfast and Nottingham to just one goal. After working with the players for three or four months, you could see they had confidence and had gelled as a team. On a level playing field we could compete and beat the rest. It was probably the toughest year in my career, that's for sure.

We may have finished bottom of the pile, with 23 points from 42 games, but we pushed all the teams very close. Belfast took the title, with Newcastle second, followed by Nottingham, Coventry, Cardiff, Sheffield and Basingstoke. Most of them had budgets far in excess of our own, and we very nearly took that seventh spot on the last weekend, missing out in an overtime loss to Belfast.

In the playoffs, we faced Belfast, Coventry and Cardiff in Group A. It was always going to be a tough group and I knew we had to be at our very best to progress. But beforehand the job was made that little bit harder as most of the team came down with a mystery illness. A virus floored some of the guys for around two to three weeks, which meant we couldn't train properly. Sometimes in practice we couldn't actually do anything because there were only six or seven guys there! Hardly the best preparation for the quality of the Devils, Giants and Blaze. I also got tonsillitis! But that's the game, I suppose.

The schedule, unlike the previous year, was kind to us – we faced all three of our opponents at home first, over the space of a week, and then travelled away. In our first game against Cardiff we lost 1-4, but played pretty well for most of the game. Frustratingly, we were one up and seemingly cruising for forty minutes before they scored and we fell apart. It wasn't a particularly tough game at all and I felt we could have got something out of it if we kept our composure. But they got the chance and scored three in quick succession.

That proved to be the story of our playoffs. We gave our all, but while we were getting six or seven chances and not putting them away, the opposition only needed one or two. After that Devils defeat, it was always going to be tough.

Belfast were next up and again we were in the game, at 2-3, and we had them on the rack but went down 2-4. A day later our challenge was ended with a 2-5 home defeat to the Blaze. The final three games finished 2-10 (Blaze), 3-3 (Belfast) and 2-5 (Cardiff). For the record, Newcastle won the playoff final at the NIC against Sheffield 2-1.

People have asked whether Edinburgh should have come up to the Elite League, and I have to admit there were times when I wondered where the next win would come from. But, on the whole, I would say it was a success. Edinburgh scrapped and fought to take points from most teams and made the transition from bottom of the semi-pro BNL to competing against the 'big boys'.

The Caps also took the top teams to a single goal and that is something the team couldn't have done a few years back. Now the management has to take the club to the next level. If it doesn't maximise on what it has learnt during that first season, it will struggle every year. If it doesn't build, the sponsors and fans will lose out. But it's tough – the other teams have big sponsors and rinks compared to Murrayfield. The Capitals' sponsors are great, don't get me wrong, but they aren't in the same league financially as Coors for example. Edinburgh needs a major sponsor with serious money as it could make all the difference. The decision to move up to the Elite has been vindicated in my view and I hope the club has it within itself to move forward.

On the ice, I don't think some of the fans appreciated the size of the task ahead of the Caps at the beginning of the season and how far the team went during the year. The budget was limited and we tried to get as much out of it as possible. Perhaps if some of the teams had stuck to the cap we could have done better. Some of the guys had to supplement their hockey careers with other jobs, so it was difficult to get any sort of continuity. But that's what they and we could afford. It was tough for me and I have no doubts that it was tough for the players too.

I took some stick on the Internet in the early days too, but the team wasn't that bad and didn't deserve the criticism it got. Someone put a poll on the official website asking whether I should resign or not – and that was in the early days of the season! I knew the team's limitations and perhaps some of the fans didn't realise that. I knew there was a lot of work in it and it was always going to take two or three months to get going.

We were unfortunate with injuries too. If we had been sat there with eleven imports and a full complement of Brits I'm sure we would have been fine and done a lot better. But when you are sat there with six to seven guys, it was always going to be tough – especially with a line made up of guys from the Scottish National League. Some of them had never played at the top level and even struggled in the BNL. But every team has its hard luck stories. Realistically, my team needed to play out of their skins to beat the others. We just didn't have the quality so had to have the maximum effort per game to win. We also showed, especially in our excellent January, that once the roster had adjusted to life in the top flight it could pick up points.

It was a tough year but an experience I wouldn't change for the world.

25

'DREAM TEAMS...'

It is amazing in a playing career spanning the best part of twenty-five years how many players of differing calibres, nationalities and characters I have come into contact with. I'm often asked who are the best and most dangerous guys I have played alongside and faced during my playing days and it is certainly difficult to select individuals.

But after much head scratching, here are two lines of the best players I have played alongside as well as the best I have faced. I have also chosen the line I would put together if I had all the money in the world and a time machine! I have split the 'with' and 'against' into two lines to get them into my roster. These aren't necessarily the lines I would play them in! They were all first-liners in my eyes.

Hopefully they would have room for me.

Played alongside:

LINE I

Netminder

The best guy I have played with for shot stopping has to be **Geoff Sarjeant** from my days at Ayr. He was an excellent goaltender who could handle the puck really well.

Defencemen

Despite the controversial end to his hockey career in this country, **Scott Young** (Ayr and Dundee) would be the first name on my team sheet purely down to his character and passion. He had natural ability – as good as I've seen from a D man. Joining him would be **Roman Gavalier** from my days at Belfast. He never made a mistake and was the ultimate professional. He did the little things right and was a superb and solid defenceman. A lot of people didn't see the work he did, but he was superb for the Giants all year. No, he didn't score a lot of points, but he wasn't flashy and did everything right.

Forwards

Ed Courtenay would be my first choice. I played with him at Sheffield and Ayr and he is a natural hockey player. Sometimes people say hockey is difficult to play but it all came so natural to Eddie. Playing with him was simple because he really understood the game. I have always been a playmaker so found guys like Eddie easy to play with. **Jason Lafreniere** (Sheffield) was a great player. He played in the NHL with Quebec Nordiques, New York Rangers and the Tampa Bay Lightning and was solid and very reliable. **Chris Palmer** (Murrayfield and Edinburgh) was an out-and-out goalscorer who was solid like Jason and I related to him really well.

LINE 2

Netminder

Like Geoff, **Martin Klempa** (Belfast) was a pure shot stopper. His patience was as good as you will ever see. Although he couldn't handle the puck well, like most European goalies, he would be 'square' to every shot and he kept us in so many games during the 2004/05 season.

Defencemen

Swede **Martin Wiita** (Dundee) was somebody who I lavished praise on when I was coach of the Stars. He had an exceptional talent and he played on the D for us as well as going up front on many occasions. He was an unbelievable D man with phenomenal skill for such a small guy, but he was strong as an ox. **Johan Silfwerplatz** played with me in Ayr and he was an all-round defenceman who was solid week in, week out. He never made mistakes and could be relied on each game to give his all. When you can trust players like Johan, your job is a lot easier. One thing I'll never forget him doing is splitting my ear with a shot! Although I'm only allowed two defencemen per line, as it's my book, and in case of injuries, I would have **Jan Mikel** (Ayr and Dundee) as back-up.

Forwards

John Newberry played for the Montreal Canadiens and that class really came through when he joined me at Murrayfield in 1992. He was a guy who was on the same wavelength as me and we had chemistry on the ice that made the difference. When **David Longstaff** (Sheffield) was at his best, he was undoubtedly one of the best players ever to play in Britain over the last ten years. He could have made the NHL and would have had a good career there too. **George Awada** would be my third choice. He scored goals for fun with me at Belfast, and he would be constantly moving and skating to create space for you. He was a great puck winner.

And so to those I played against:

LINE I

Netminder

Frank Pietrangelo (Manchester Storm) was an amazing netminder who was really difficult to score against.

Defencemen

Kris Miller (Manchester Storm) was good as was **Greg Kuznik** (Fife). Both these guys were similar as they were exceptional on the D and skated really well.

Forwards

Adam Calder (Coventry) was dangerous as was ex-NHLer **Theo Fleury** when he iced for Belfast Giants in 2005/06. **Jason Ruff** (Belfast Giants) is also a great player.

LINE 2

Netminder

Mike Minard (Belfast) is as good a keeper as you will ever see in this country. He is a real classy guy who should have been given a regular stint at an NHL club.

Defencemen:

Troy Neumeier (Manchester Storm) was unbelievably hard to play against as were many of the NHL guys that came over during the player strike in 2004/05. One of them was the Boston Bruins' **Ian Moran** who iced for the Nottingham Panthers. He was as tough as they came. You could tell that he had played the game at the highest level.

Forwards

Going back to my earlier days, **Garry Unger** (Dundee Rockets, Peterborough Pirates) when he arrived in Britain in 1985 to play for the Dundee Rockets was superb, as was **Rick Brebant** (Durham Wasps, Cardiff Devils, Nottingham Panthers, Newcastle Cobras, Manchester Storm, London Knights, Sheffield Steelers, Manchester Phoenix) who had a great ability to keep his level up year in, year out. He was such a tenacious player. Newcastle's **Paul Ferone** is never going to win a scoring race, but he's the sort of guy that every coach needs in their team. He's tough and level-headed on the ice, but he doesn't go around and play the role – he fights the tough guys and because of that he has the respect of the players. Newcastle would have been lost without him.

Next up is the 'I'm dreaming' line-up!

Netminder

Dominik Hasek would be my keeper as his saves were first class. Perhaps he wasn't the best puck handler ever, but his saving ability was unbelievable.

Defencemen

Nicklas Lidstrom from the Detroit Red Wings would be first up. I have never seen anyone who could play as smooth as him. No one could pass the puck and control the game in the way he does. **Ray Bourque** would be next in because he was a top player and a top defenceman in the NHL year in, year out. I really admired him because he spent so long at the Boston Bruins where he dominated. His heart was there. I was very happy when he won the Stanley Cup with the Colorado Avalanche. You could see he was cut up leaving Boston, but I'm glad he got a chance to grab a ring. I'm sure the Boston fans were made up too. He is an ambassador for the sport and above that his point scoring and playmaking was out of this world.

FORWARDS

First up is very simple. **Wayne Gretzky** (Edmonton Oilers, Los-Angeles Kings, St Louis Blues, New York Rangers), the Great One. He scored more than 3,000 points in the best league in the world. He was truly the best player ever to have played the sport. Second up is **Joe Sakic** (Quebec Nordiques, Colorado Avalanche). He is one of those guys who has just been at the top of their game everywhere he's iced. Finally, **Mark Messier** (Edmonton Oilers, New York Rangers, Vancouver Canucks). He is domineering, can score goals, passes well, fights like the best of them, as well as checks and could get his team pumped up better than anyone.

It's tough to answer a question on how I would coach these guys (I thank Mike Appleton for posing that one!) but one thing is for sure: they wouldn't take much work. I think you would need to make sure they were on the same page, but they would be able to read each other's minds as the chemistry would be certainly there. There is so much offence in that line that it would intimidate and frighten other teams.

As for a 'home' arena, they would play at the Odyssey in Belfast, because the ice surface and the complete package there is superb, with Sheffield Arena as back-up/training ice!

26

'PLAYING THE PERCENTAGES...'

At the first training camp in Edmonton, general manager Glen Sather said I was the smartest player there other than Wayne Gretzky. This was a great comment on my abilities, as well as a honour, and even to this day I'm proud that he said it about me. He was talking about my ability to read the ice and know what is going on around me. People often ask how I seem to be able to understand what is happening on ice and I have to say that it is a counting game. It is that simple. Ice hockey is not a tough sport to play if you know how to read the situation and take the right action. But all players make the game look hard sometimes!

It's difficult to explain how I 'see' the game on the ice as a player and coach, but as a playmaker I believe it is vital to read what is going on instead of firing off a wayward pass or shot. That is how I have gained my points over the years. First and foremost as a coach my teams always go into a game with the attitude of trying to win it. What I mean is that I have never sent one of my teams out there with the intention of playing for a draw (like you can get in football) or intentionally to injure another team. I have always wanted to play in and coach a fair team, that plays fluent hockey without guys in the penalty box.

Deep down I have to admit I don't actually find the game that difficult to play. The thing I have always struggled with is the physical aspect of it. I am 5ft 10in and around 180 pounds and I can't out-muscle guys who are bigger and taller than me. That doesn't mean I still do not try! Sometimes I have tried, and it can work, but over the years I have asked myself if there really is any point wasting energy trying to take the puck off these guys when it might not happen for me. What's the point in trying to fight for it?

I ask myself this because I have always tried to play the game smart by playing the percentages. It's not rocket science – I do not try and give the puck away stupidly or take on a situation that might mean losing the puck or the advantage. It isn't copping out, it is taking the 'easier' option on the ice to create a play. If you have the puck it is better for the opposition to try and get it off you so you can capital-ise on their mistakes.

With the puck you have to make an influential play or try and cre-ate a scoring chance. There's no point just dumping it in and letting them come back at you. Losing the puck is like saying, 'Go on, you take a shot'. You can't say, 'I don't feel comfortable with the puck, so I will just pass it' – every pass should make a difference. Of course, in some circumstances you may be camped in your D and the last option, and it has to be the last one, is to fire it out and clear your lines.

Dumping it in is a last option to me. I have been lucky to play in some big rinks that have allowed me to carry it over the blue line, but some coaches do like the puck being dumped in to put pressure on the opposition. I do not like that tactic at all. In my view you should always try and keep hold of it. If you have the puck, they can-not score. Simple.

With the puck I am looking to drag an opposition player out of position to make a play, but some hockey players these days don't seem to have the patience to do that. They will see a guy come towards them and they will get rid of the puck straightaway. By wait-ing that split-second further you can choose a pass that can open up the ice. If you panic, you will rush the play and lose it. I am playing a numbers game every time I am on or off the puck. If we are in our end and I pick up the puck, I am not worried about who is in front or alongside, but who is behind me. Why? So I can speed up, slow down to bring other players into play or take a player on.

Choosing to go one-on-one with a player is something I would rather not do as it is a low percentage play. Ask yourself, what are the chances of getting past them with the puck? Is it fifty-fifty? I believe you do not have to take a player on to make a play – passing to a player in space can make all the difference instead. If an opposing player has fallen over in our end, either near the net or in the corner, I know with one pass we can outnumber them in their zone. I also know which defenceman in our team will be free to come down the ice. That is done by just taking that split-second to see what is going on around you.

The thing you have to worry about as a coach is odd-man rushes. If a team is coming at you three-on-two you are in trouble. If you have the rush, with an opposition player down, you can bring your free defenceman into play to make that scoring chance. In the end, that is what it is all about. At lot of my goals and points have come by seeing this position and waiting for my defenceman to come up and help out the play. You do this by holding onto the puck, slowing down and waiting for them to join – if you feel that a scoring chance can be created by doing it.

One thing I can do is tell where that 'special' play is going to come from to set up a scoring chance probably two passes before it happens. If I have the puck I instinctively know coming over the red line if my team will have a scoring chance by simply analysing the numbers. If that opening isn't there, it is a low percentage play and you can dump it in and put the pressure back on them. If players can slow down to react to the play they can create these chances. Over the years I have been fortunate to do this, but it does get harder with better defenders and netminders these days.

Another thing to think about is who the player is you are passing to. To create a genuine scoring chance the player has to be able to fire off a shot straight away and not handle the puck to get into position. Because, if a guy has to handle the puck to set themselves up, the moment could be lost. You have to make sure that when it is passed, the guy can shoot the puck straightaway. I see it all the time – guys pass to others but don't take into account what foot his colleague shoots off, or what hand. They just want to pass it really quick.

Although I am trying to explain how I see the game, this isn't something I have learnt. There are many players better than me out there, but I have never sat and watched the game and looked at how this is done. Obviously I have worked hard on the ice and in the gym, but as for making the play at the right time, or nailing a pass, I just don't know how I do it. It was just the way I developed as a player.

You learn that it is best not to do things. Does that makes sense? You learn what not to do, and therefore you learn to do the things you are supposed to do, by not doing the things you are not! Some players cannot get their heads around this and will just pass the puck blind or throw it away. You do the smart things and have the poise to make the right choice. I try not to rush when I am on the puck and have a level head. It doesn't always come off but by and large it has been fine. When you are playing you should be trying to give yourself as much time as possible so you can make the play.

This isn't something you can teach though. The player must get the basics right first but I do think you need to have it 'upstairs' to get it right. I see this with lots of hockey players who try that amazing pass and lose the puck. If some had more poise it could make all the difference.

It is also important to say that playing the percentages isn't about being a safe or boring player. It is about making the right choices – if you see a guy open you should pass to him, not to the guy with two people around them. Passing the puck to a moving player is a lot easier than trying to take a player on. Non-moving players are totally useless to me.

So with all this in mind and going back to if I have the puck in my zone and I am coming up the ice, my first thought is to see how many guys I have got with me and how many the opposition has in front. Let's use the three-on-two example. The next thing I do is not to look at the opposition! I look to see who my next guy is and if they are any use to me – and these are usually the guys behind me. Then I have to see how the three-on-two could become a two-on-one by taking one of the defencemen out.

Ninety-nine times out of 100 I will take the puck over the blue line as this opens up the zone and gives me more options. You do see lots of players passing over the blue line but that goes against the percentages. Some guys don't use it to their advantage and I firmly believe that getting in their zone opens it up and you don't get caught for offside. A simple pass to the right or left could take one D out. Then the next pass is crucial – who is the player that is going to shoot? Are they left- or right-handed? Do they like it on, between or in front of their skates? Knowing this means you can line up the pass. The thing is, all this can happen within seconds. It can take only four seconds to get from your zone to theirs! Good luck...

I have scored a lot of points by examining the play in this way and perhaps this is now a good time to respond to the stick I get about claiming assists! Being told I have got points for goals I have had no hand in is something I am used to. It started as a laugh but has continued as a running joke. I have to say that I have never heard anything so ridiculous in my life! These days the referees do not just give assists to anyone. When I was young I might have claimed a few, but every player has had assists that they don't deserve. It seems that people are always looking for an angle on a sportsman at the top. Players don't hassle the ref to gain points they haven't earned. I have told referees in the past that I didn't touch it, but still gained the point. Once I even contacted the league to make sure that a player got a point they deserved. But people don't see that side.

Some people treat it like you get thirty a season! Of course you will get points sometimes that you don't deserve, but you will also lose out on a few. The whole thing wears a bit thin these days. Have I been wrongly awarded 2,000 of my nearly 4,000 career points? No. I have to say that I do not actually care what people think of me. I have a job to do and that is that.

27

'YOU EFFECTIVELY LEAD TWO DIFFERENT LIVES...'

So, you've played all year and the season is over. As I have said earlier, you can either have around five months celebrating a famous playoff win, or a long time commiserating. As a coach, things are slightly different, as you are always planning ahead. When the season finally finishes and you take your kit off for the last time, it's actually a big relief. Seven and a half months have passed and you can give your body a rest.

I'm sure people do not realise how much ice hockey actually takes out of you over the year. Physically, you lose a lot of energy and muscle and mentally you are shattered. Throughout most of my career, and especially towards the end of it, I have always given myself two or three weeks' rest. I will avoid training in this time. Then, after the rehabilitation, I will start lifting weights. This is probably why I always seem to have more muscle during the off-season too!

I have never really lifted weights during the season, perhaps because I have always trained around three times a week and I've felt my body didn't need the extra work. Certainly, as I have got older, the games have taken a lot out of me and I feel tired after a weekend's fixtures. Sometimes it is tough to train so I lay off putting in the extra strain of weightlifting in the gym. During the off-season, after my rest I will hit the gym five or six times a week to get myself ready for new season. For anyone in sport, staying in shape on your 'holidays' is vital and at my age I need to make sure I keep the weight off. But stopping for those first few weeks is a nightmare as you notice the pain and the tweaks in your muscles. It's also the same with playing for the first couple of weeks. Sometimes I think, 'How am I going to get through the season?' but you get into the groove.

In the off-season I spend a lot of time with my family because I don't see them that much. At the weekends you are always busy so it is important to spend as much time with them as possible. You effectively lead two different lives during the campaign – an on-ice and an off-ice life. On the ice everything is devoted to the game and striving to be the best; off it, you have to be devoted to keeping in shape. Because if you don't go to the gym, not matter what you eat, you will put on weight. It is important to keep right into it. When I eventually stop playing, I will still keep in shape because it is some-thing you never lose – it's in your blood. I cannot see myself in the gym when I am seventy though!

Most of the players I know go on holiday, but I don't go abroad these days. If you go for too long it is difficult to get back into it. My favourite holiday destination is definitely Las Vegas. I have been a few times and you can do what you want. You can play cards, it has great hotels, and there is so much you can do. I like that sort of stuff! I do go away every year with my sister-in-law Nicola and her husband Neil McKay, and all our kids.

What people might not realise is that I do not go on the ice for around four months until mid-August! I think it is important just to be away for a bit and do something different. I also feel I don't need to skate as I keep in shape. I run around Arthur's Seat in Edinburgh, which is a beautiful extinct volcano, with my brother-in-law and it's something I really enjoy as it keeps up my stamina. I also play a lot of golf.

I have to admit I am a golf addict. Melissa knows when I have a game on at my local club, Archerfield, because I am pumped up and she can't wait until I leave the house. Myself and Melvyn Strang play against Charlie Philp and Mark Noble and we certainly have a strong rivalry. In fact, I like nothing better than to beat those guys! I also like to walk my dog Rudi and to feed the ducks, swans and wildlife down by my local river. I'm there most days and it's like a religion to me. I am an animal lover. There are also two or three hockey schools to teach so I keep really busy.

As all this is going on, I am recruiting my team for the next season. This happens all year round, but intensifies over the summer months. People think the season starts in September but it's all year round, checking players and negotiating and getting the balance is really hard. If there's one thing I have learnt, if you don't get your close season right, it can be a heck of a long campaign!

28

'THE LEAGUES NEED TO WORK TOGETHER...'

A quarter of a century is a long time to be involved in any sport. Like many others, ice hockey has seen an immense amount of change and is vastly different from those early days when I first stepped out on to the Murrayfield ice aged fourteen. First and foremost, I have to say that the game is in a much better state than it was a few years ago. But it hasn't been easy to get this far.

We always seem to make the same mistakes year in, year out and I think this legacy has held back the game's development. I'm mainly referring to how much a team is allowed to spend. In the top flight over the years the teams have spent amazing amounts of cash on players and we have lost teams from the league as a result. Just look back at the Superleague. We lost London, Bracknell, Manchester and Ayr from the league and were very close to seeing Sheffield disappear altogether. That club was in turmoil. Towards the back end of Superleague, you didn't know what was going to happen and who would survive until the end of the season. That trend started to reverse when Coventry came into the BNL and then the Elite League. It showed everyone how a successful club could be run on and off the ice.

To stop clubs falling by the wayside and to improve our game we need to reduce the amount of imports. In the Elite League in

2005/06, you had eleven import slots per team. With eight teams that's eighty-eight players that are 'imported labour'. There's no way we can build for the future if there are that many in the league. As a coach I understand why teams are reluctant to drop the level. If they do they will have to pay the 'excess' for the British guys – especially the top home-grown players. As things stand, if they look abroad they can bring in an import of the same quality sometimes on a cheaper wage. Yes, it's a quick fix – the talent is already there and it doesn't need to be nurtured. But if we were to reduce the number of imports permitted there would be more money to spend on quality overseas guys. And it would stop clubs, providing the wage cap stayed the same, having to find that final import on a pittance. What the public don't understand is that we don't pay top dollar anymore in this country. Years ago we did, and we had fewer imports. So there are pros and cons to it. I would like to reduce the level but not at a great rate. You need to be able to bleed it into the system so you can see what happens. And I am sure that with fewer imports there need be no reduction in quality, sponsorship or attendance. That's why I was glad that for the new season, 2006/07, the EIHL have reduced the level to ten.

What any reduction does is give a boost to the British guy who realises he may have a chance of making the top two lines. It gives them a goal to improve themselves. Up at Edinburgh I had to work with the British guys and it was only halfway through the season when I saw real improvement. Making the 'line to the ice' very clear by reducing imports may give these guys an extra kick up the backside.

I know coaches are under pressure to get results so the first thing they will do is play an import but I do see the tide changing, especially from talking to others in the league. Just a reduction of one per team removes ten imports and that is a start. There is a long way to go but perhaps we should plan for the next five years instead of debating what the rules should be yearly. Initially, I would like to see it stay at ten, then as we bring the Brits on, reduce it by one a year. Ten is fine; it is ample for the league's teams.

I know some are worried that if we include more British players or drop the import level the standard will decrease. In Superleague there were sixteen to seventeen imports, which was far too high, but they were creating a new league and therefore wanted a very high standard. But teams were struggling. If the Elite League was competing against another league on the same import footing, then it would be understandable. There is a happy medium and we are very close to it. If we could reduce it once a year for five years, that would be great.

Sadly, the teams don't have the infrastructure anymore to bring the kids on and take advantage of the changing league. It's true that most of the teams have smaller clubs in their areas, but don't utilise them. This all goes back to the import level; with eleven or so imports, as it was, and with some games played with just two lines the British guys don't get a chance. It's all about trying to win, but if everyone began to play the same proportion of Brits, wouldn't it be a more level playing field?

A league and a sport saturated with imports has had a knock-on effect on the national team. With more imports came less ice time for the young Brits. When I played in Pool A, a large proportion of the team were on dual passports. This stifled the opportunities for the kids to get into the team and when the 'duals' left, Great Britain struggled. Only now are we starting to get the team back on an even keel and that is through a young British team. The old stalwarts have gone and the youngsters have come through. But how should we improve? The first thing we need to do is find the right coaching and give them the backing. Then we need to select a level the team is comfortable with. What I mean is, do we decide we are a Pool A team or Pool B? If it's the former then we need to dedicate our league and national programmes to getting and staying there. Realistically, we shouldn't aim too high, because the league structure in this country is not set up to compete with the likes of Canada and Russia.

As a nation we are looking to be Pool A all the time and perhaps in 1994 we were overachieving a little. One thing for sure is that when we played the likes of the Soviets and the Italians, we had little preparation and got our arses kicked. We literally turned up at the airport after the playoffs and were on our way to the tournament. With no time beforehand, it is difficult for a team to gel, but I can understand why the players cannot meet up earlier due to league commitments.

To be realistic, for the time being, we have to say we are a middle-of-the-table Pool B team. Of course, I would love to be wrong and dream we could get to Pool A again, but it's a number of years off in my view. Pool B is also a tough pool to stay in and so perhaps we should be proud to say we are there. The teams that go to the World Championships will take three or four weeks off to have a shot at promotion. For us, it's a few days and as a result we are not prepared. The talent is there for all to see though, and the team traditionally gets stronger as it progresses through the tournament. With a little more preparation, who knows what could happen? It's tough on the players, coaches and organisers to get the squad playing to its full ability after only a few days. They go there with 100 per cent commitment and loads of passion to do well, but don't have warm-up games like the other teams and it shows. The coaches need more time with their players.

It's good to see lots of good young players coming through. The Great Britain Under-18s recently won the gold medal and the Under-21s have a great team so the foundations are there.

Has imported talent turned kids off the sport? Possibly. There have been a lot of young and talented players leave ice hockey because they could not get the ice time. Of the GB Junior team I played with in 1981, hardly any of them were still playing in the late eighties. Personally, I think you need to show kids the way into the top teams through the right infrastructure at club level, but also in the different age category leagues as well.

I think there should be a British league where the Under-19s from Scotland would take on England and Wales. This would take lots of interaction from the difference league bodies. But even in

Scotland, some teams have Under-11s and other Under-12s and they can't compete against each other. Each team should have the same structure and be in the same boat. But that is up to the governing bodies to sort out. They need to say that we are going to plan for the next five or ten years and get these structures sorted. Perhaps we are neglecting the sport by planning for one year in advance. It doesn't make much sense. The league bodies tend to fix a problem when it turns up, but not in the long term. For the British kids to get better and the GB team to make the Olympics and Pool A, the EIHL, EPL and SNL need to come together to sort out the sport's future. You have to ask who is running the sport at the moment.

So do I fancy the GB job? There was talk of myself taking it on but it never materialised and to be honest, I wasn't offered it anyway. I think it is a labour of love and I wish Paul Thompson all the best. If they get to Pool A and the Olympics, well done. I'm not ruling myself out of doing it; you should never say never, but it's one of those jobs that would be enjoyable but tough!

One positive thing about hockey at present is that there are a lot of intelligent owners these days who are thinking about the business. The days of John Nike and Bill Barr have gone now – they were spending fortunes on their teams and, let's be honest, they could have got their teams for a lot less. The future is good. Neil Black at Nottingham is a prime example. He's canny and he leads the Panthers very well. He looks after the business and lets the general manager and coaches get on with it. Like most of the owners in the league he is very shrewd and that means there will be hockey in these teams for the next twenty or thirty years. Neil is a good role model for the league. You never hear him in the papers unless it's really serious. The leagues need people like that if they are going to be strong. I wouldn't want to tempt fate, but I believe the days of losing two teams during a season are long gone.

I'd like to see sponsorship, more advertising and have the game on television more consistently than it has been. Finding a major league sponsor is vital; the signing of bmibaby is a good start. We haven't had one since the days of Heineken and Sekonda and I think it's important for the identity of the teams to have that. For some of the teams it is still a struggle and there is a fine line between success and failure. Some certainly have to be very grateful for the unsung heroes – the security guys, people who put the nets out and the volunteers. Teams need a lot of help from these guys to be successful. Without them, they would have additional worries on top of their usual overheads; the houses, cars and travel. It's a tough sport to succeed in. In some teams it is still very tight if they lose a couple of fixtures to poor ice, rescheduling or something else, especially if you have hired the rink. You still have to pay and you lose your gate.

It is all bad though? Of course not. If there's one thing I had to pick out it would be that the standard is much better over the twenty-five years or so I have been playing. When I started, it was three imports and a bunch of Brits skating about and we were eating fish suppers before a game! Now we stay over at hotels the night before and have proper pre-match meals. Suggest that to an owner back then and they would have hit the roof. Yes, the costs are higher now but so is professionalism and look at the players we are attracting. Theo Fleury is an NHL superstar. The level has improved fourfold at least.

I wouldn't say the game is more important than it was back then, there's just a lot more pressure on the teams, coaches and players. The players are paid a lot and have to be professional. For some, it is a full-time job. There has to be pressure – it goes with the territory. For the owners, choosing the wrong personnel could be curtains. It can damage their businesses. And the pressure is immense – I have seen players and coaches crack up because of it. It is 'just a game' and I wouldn't like to see people's health affected because of it. Of course, it's not as fun as it used to be because it is a lot harder to play! I still love it though. Back when I started out it was a laugh, and it still is now, but with more pressure. If you don't enjoy playing, you should not be playing, I suppose.

My first memories of the sport were the fantastic rivalries. Racers' games against Fife were amazing to play in and close, hotly contested rivalries are still with us. Sheffield *v*. Nottingham, Coventry *v*. Belfast – if these passions get people through the gates then it has to be good for the sport. If you create that atmosphere before the game, especially through the media, and increase ticket sales, then all the better.

After all, the public wants to be entertained. It wants goals, hits and fights, atmosphere and intensity. If fans turn up and it is mundane, they will not come again. Hockey has a reputation to fulfil. I'm a firm believer that there's always a place for rivalry as long as it doesn't take over the game. The fans' abuse of Theo Fleury when he was over here created some very negative press but caused a ticket rush for his next appearance. Is that what we want to be creating? Perhaps it wasn't the greatest advert for the sport.

When you look at ice hockey and rivalries, personalities are important. Simmsy is certainly one who can create this. He sits up in the Whitehouse at Sheffield's rink and winds up other teams and the fans love it. He can be close to the bone and sometimes I say to him, 'What are you saying that for?' He also uses his column in the trade press to have a go at other teams (namely Nottingham) and certainly creates an atmosphere. It's tongue in cheek – sure, people don't like it, but it isn't that bad. He does get it back though. I phoned him up to chant 'easy, easy' when Sheffield got beat by Basingstoke and their announcer was sticking it to him. It was funny!

As for the physical game itself, the future is bright. The product on the ice is pretty high at the moment. We could probably do with changing a few things, such as making the lines a bit bigger to reduce offsides and stop keepers from playing the puck. Fighting should also go to the NHL standard five-minute penalty for one scrap and a game misconduct for the second in my view.

A combined league would also be great, but unless we reduce our imports to come in line with the EPL it will never happen. Perhaps a happy medium could be created of around six for all teams, but it is unlikely. There is too big a gulf between the EPL and EIHL. I would like to see it happen as it would make sense for one big league, but the arena teams are just too big. Some have 6,000 people attending and others 300. It just wouldn't work.

Yes, hockey has problems, but it's in a good state. Let's now move it to the next level.

29

'I'M LOOKING FORWARD
TO THE FUTURE…'

I've spent twenty-five years playing hockey and at this moment, thinking about the future, it is no clearer to me than it was when I took the ice for the first time in a senior game. At fourteen years of age I just wanted to play. I have never set targets, been that ambitious or been one to set goals. So, as I write this final chapter, I haven't made a decision on my *playing* future, but know I will be continuing for another year or two. 2006/07 will probably be my final year.

In terms of *coaching*, I'm looking forward to a good year with the Manchester Phoenix. Leaving Edinburgh was hard, it is my home-town club, after all, but any job I take has to be suitable to my needs. I enjoyed working with Scott, the fans and the players, but my family is my main priority and that will always influence what type of position I take.

At the end of the 2005/06 season it came out in the press that I was quitting the club. That never was the case. There is and was no bad blood between Scott, the club and me. I left because I wanted to win trophies and want place on record that I enjoyed my time there.

People should realise that hockey players and coaches have to pay their bills like the rest and that the sport is their livelihood. We all need to make a living. Fans wonder why players they've idolised move on to other clubs but they do not understand the circumstances. If someone comes along and offers you more money then I can completely understand why a player would move on. I have never chased the money in my career but have to look to the future now.

During the 2005/06 season I had offers from two Elite League teams, but turned them both down. One thing I will always do, no matter where I end up, is see out a season with the guys I am contracted to. Because I started the season with the Caps, despite how difficult it got during the year, I turned both offers down flat and would do so in the future.

With the import level now down to ten the British hockey player, especially the good one, becomes a valuable commodity in the league. But for my own position it will probably make no difference. For the next couple of years or so I will be coaching and playing, which means I will be in demand. The new import level is good for the Brits, but regardless of what is happening, I like to coach and build teams and that is what I want to do in the future. So the new rules do not mean I will go back to being just a player!

Of course people are beginning to wonder when I am finally going to retire from playing. I don't feel I'm ready to do it just yet and so will continue to play for another year, possibly more. I don't look that far ahead so it's one year at a time. During the 2005/06, season I asked myself if I should continue because I was tired, deflated and my own game suffered a little bit. And it is such a big job playing and coaching at the same time. But I still enjoy playing and if I stop, well, that would be it for me at this stage I think. I have been offered just coaching jobs in the past, but I really love playing and wouldn't want them.

Sometimes I feel like I just want to coach though. I can still compete at a decent and reasonable level but I know that it's part and parcel of the game that I will get sorer after matches! I am not stupid though. Already I try to pace myself during games and make sure I stay out of the rough stuff and the battles. You can't act like a twenty-one-year-old any more; it's all about being a little smarter.

As I said, I never have planned too far ahead so who knows if

2006/07 will be my final year? You never know. A lot will depend on if I am struggling on the ice or not, and if playing conflicts with my coaching duties. Although I am pretty fit at the moment, I'm sure I could be fitter and that would help. But with playing all the time it is difficult to take your fitness to the next level. I'll see how it goes.

Some guys say to me that I could play for another ten years, but I can't see it going that far. I should have stopped playing by the time I am forty, but who knows? Steve Moria is still going and he's in his forties so why not? I know I will have to stop at some point. I would like to finish at the top of my game, going out on a high with a team that could win a championship. That would be the perfect way to finish.

Coaching-wise, I have a couple of ambitions. I want to coach a team, on the right budget, that can compete at the highest level and go all the way to the Championship title. That team would be able to compete in a league where everyone was on the same level playing field. It would test the players and the coach to the limit. But overall I want to coach a team that wins things. Ideally, I would have loved to coach a big budget team in Edinburgh that could compete with the likes of Belfast, Sheffield, Coventry and Nottingham financially and on the ice, where you could go for the big-name players. I think any player or coach would like to do this in their home town. But without an influx of cash, the Capitals were never going to do that.

Yes, I have thought about coaching in the United States or Canada but the jobs are just as challenging over here! In Britain you have to be smart and recruit well at the beginning of the year to get it right. Over there, it is more flexible as you have farm teams and coaches all around you. We shouldn't underestimate how difficult it is to coach in the UK.

These are just some of the reasons why I took on the Manchester job. There is a decent budget there, which means we will hopefully be able to compete, and it will be a real challenge. It will be tough, they are building a club back up once again, but owner Neil Morris is passionate, as are the fans up there. In my meetings with him, Neil came across as a genuine guy who wants the team to do well. We built up a rapport and he came across as an honest guy.

I'm not particularly concerned about the history of hockey in the city. Yes, the Storm went under and the Phoenix mothballed but there is no reason, with the new rink being built in Altrincham, why the club cannot be successful. They have great potential.

One thing is for sure: I will probably be in hockey all my life. Over the past few years I have been wondering what to do and whether to leave the sport completely. It has been a tiring few years and I have been drained. I have spoke to friends and my wife about it, but when it gets to the summer I can't wait for it to begin again. It's in your blood and you're counting down the days. At the end of the season, you're glad it's over, but after a couple of days you want to get going again. The season should be longer in my view!

If I am purely coaching, that might be different of course. When I'm sixty-five I can see myself behind a bench or desk and I'm sure it will still be as enjoyable as it has been. I am always learning, using videos, research and the Internet so I'm sure I will be a better coach then. I'm looking forward to the future!

When I eventually do hang up my skates, I would like to be remembered as a hockey player that gave many people a lot of enjoyment. I hope the fans enjoyed watching me, respected me and saw someone who was an honest guy. I would hope I am a role model for youngsters to look up to.

There will be better players than me come along. Although I am not classing myself in the same bracket, there will always be people like Pelé and The Great One who probably will never be bettered. But there will be players who will come through and dominate in the same way they did. In Britain, there will be another Tony Hand.

Personally in the future, I would love to be able to break par at golf. It would be a great day. I would also love to travel to take in a safari or something like that. I'm not very ambitious. My main goal is to look after my family.

As for my epitaph, it would simply read: 'British Ice Hockey – Assisted by Tony Hand'.

QUOTES

'We formed a great understanding, but I haven't seen many players that haven't formed such an understanding with Tony. He makes people around him better. He is immense.' – Ivan Matulik

'He would make a real good referee. He has eyes like a hawk. Referees have to be on the top of the game as he is always watching!' – Moray Hanson

'Tony's record speaks for itself. He is a real ambassador on the ice. When it comes to playmaking there are not many better than him.' – Rick Brebant

'Tony Hand was one of the greatest players ever to play for or against the Steelers, he has been both a credit to the sport and an inspiration to all British players over a twenty-year spell. Tony's best asset isn't his awareness or puck-handling skills; it is his great competitiveness, his desire and will to win. Tony Hand has that "fuck you" mentality that so many people don't have. It helps take him to a level others can only dream of.' – Dave Simms

'At the training camp I could see that he had a great ability to read the ice and he was the smartest player there other than Wayne Gretzky. He skated well, his intelligence on the ice really stood out. He was a real prospect.' – Glen Sather

'He is the top sportsman of his generation and the greatest ambassador UK hockey has ever had. He has given a lot of people happiness over the years and made a few of his mates very miserable too!' – Paul Thompson

'I would need another chapter in this book to recall all the great times I've had with Tony... he is an extraordinary player, a natural leader, a genuine ambassador for the game and a great friend.' – Les Lovell

'The first time I saw Tony was at the public skating sessions in Murrayfield when he was about nine years old. He was one of the smallest kids out there, but no one could catch him. Big lads used to chase him around the rink but they couldn't get close! The whole focus when I went to Scotland was to develop kids in hockey but also develop them to be good citizens and nice young men. I think Tony epitomises that whole thing.' – Alex Dampier

'I always describe Tony to other people as a freak as I cannot fathom why he is as good as he is considering the state hockey has been in over the years in the UK. I mean, it isn't exactly high on the list of sporting agendas in the country is it? I am in awe of how he has learnt to play the game on his own. I have been fortunate to play with some good players over the years and as a winger/goalscorer I needed a good playmaker to set me up. Over my seventeen years of hockey Tony is in my top three players... that's how good he is. Some of my fondest memories in the sport are of playing on a line with Tony in Sheffield.' – Ed Courtenay

HONOURS AND AWARDS

INTERNATIONAL — SENIOR GB HONOURS

Year	Honour	Pool	Country
1989	Bronze Medal	Pool D	Belgium
1990	Gold Medal	Pool D	Wales
1992	Gold Medal	Pool C	England
1993	Gold Medal	Pool B	Holland
1999	Silver Medal	Pool B	Denmark
2000	Bronze Medal	Pool B	Poland
2001	Silver Medal	Pool B	Slovenia

DOMESTIC MAJOR TROPHIES

Year	Honour
1985/86	Heineken British Championship Murrayfield Racers)
1985/86	Norwich Union Cup (Murrayfield Racers)
1986/87	Heineken British League (Murrayfield Racers)
1987/88	Heineken British League (Murrayfield Racers)
1989/90	Norwich Union Cup (Murrayfield Racers)

1993/94	Benson & Hedges Cup (Murrayfield Racers)
1995/96	Benson & Hedges Cup (Sheffield Steelers)
1995/96	British Championship (Sheffield Steelers)
1995/96	Heineken British League (Sheffield Steelers)
1996/97	Sekonda Superleague Playoffs (Sheffield Steelers)
1998/99	Sekonda Challenge Cup (Sheffield Steelers)
2001/02	Findus British National League (Dundee Stars)
2001/02	Findus British National League Championship (Dundee Stars)
2004/05	British National Crossover Cup (Belfast Giants)

OTHER AWARDS AND ACCOLADES

Year	Honour
1985/86	Young British Player of the Year
1986/87	BIHWA Team of the Year
	BIHWA British All-Star
1987/88	BIHWA Team of the Year
	BIHWA British All-Star
1988/89	BIHWA Team of the Year
	BIHWA British All-Star
	BIHWA Player of the Year
1989/90	BIHWA Team of the Year
	Players' Player of the Year
	Golden Helmet Award (All-Time Top League Scorer)
	Most Valuable Player, Pool D, Wales
1991/92	BIHWA All-Star Team
	Players' Player of the Year
	Leading Scorer
	Pool C – Best Forward
1992/93	BIHWA All-Star Team
	Players' Player of the Year
1993/94	BIHWA All-Star Team
1994/95	BIHWA All-Star Team

1995/96	Players Player of the Year
	Top League Points Scorer
	BIHWA All-Star Team
	European Cup Player of the Tournament.
1997/98	BIHWA All-Star Second Team
1998/99	Top British Scorer
1999/00	Top British Scorer
2000/01	Division One, Slovenia – All-Star Team
	BIHWA Sekonda Superleague First Team
	Top British Scorer
2001/02	Division One, Hungary – All-Star Team
	Top Points Scorer
	BIHWA All-Star Team (BNL)
	Player of the Year
	Coach of the Year
2002/03	BIHWA All-Star First Team (BNL)
2003/04	BIHWA All-Star Team (BNL)
2004/05	BIHWA Elite League All-Star Team
	BIHWA Best British Forward
	BIHWA Top British Scorer
	BIHWA Top League scorer
	BIHWA Player of the Year
	EIHL All-Star team
2005/06	BIHWA Elite League All-Star Team
	BIHWA Best British Forward
	BIHWA Top British Scorer

PLAYERS TONY HAS PLAYED WITH DOMESTICALLY

MURRAYFIELD RACERS

Alex Dampier, Andy Butts, Andy Main, Andy McLeod, Bill Sobkowich, Billy Dunbar, Bobby Hay, Brian Burley, Brian Collinson, Brian McKee, Brian Meharry, Brian Popiel, Callum Hastings, Chris Kelland, Chris Palmer, Chuck Brimmer, Craig Dickson, Darren Cunningham, Dave Dalgleish, Dave Shyiak, Dave Wilson, David Park, David Samper, David Smith, Davie Mason, Dean Edmiston, Denis Clair, Denis Paul, Derek Reilly, Dougie Moodie, Duncan McIntyre, Frank Morris, Gary Hutchinson, Gord MacDougal, Gordon Inglis, Gordon Whyte, Graham Flockhart, Grant Heaps, Grant Slater, Hugh Findlay, Ian Pound, Ian Ramsay, Jason Hannigan, Jim Lynch, Jim Mollard, Jim Pennycook, Jimmy Jack, John Ballantyne, John Hay, John Newberry, Keith Foster, Kenny Cruden, Kenny Robertson, Kevin Renton, Kyle McDonough, Larry Gaudet, Laurie Dunbar, Lawrence Lovell, Lawrie Lovell, Lee Pow, Les Lovell, Lindsay Lovell, Louis Haman, Luc Beausoleil, Mark Cole, Mark Graham, Mark Hercus, Mark McKendrick, Martin McKay, Michael Holmes, Mike Jeffrey, Mike Kelly, Mike Snell, Mike Ware, Mike Whitelaw, Moray Hanson, Neil Cunningham, Norrie Grieve, Paul Gatens, Paul Hand, Paul Heavey, Paul Myles, Paul Pentland, Richard Laplante, Richie Lamb, Rick Fera, Robert Jack, Rocky Saganiuk, Roger Hunt, Ross MacIntosh, Scott Anderson, Scott Archibald, Scott Neil, Scott Nicol, Scott Orban, Scott Plews, Scott Robertson, Steve Combe, Steve Moore, Steven Flockhart, Stevie Hunter Stuart Parker, Sylvain Naud, Tom Karalis, Willie Archibald, Willie Kerr.

EDINBURGH RACERS

Bob Korol, Chris Palmer, David Park, Dean Edmiston, Gary Hutchinson, Ivan Matulik, Jamie Airnes, John Robertson, Kevin Renton, Laurie Dunbar, Les Lovell, Marko Pieniniemi, Merv Priest, Mike Ware, Moray Hanson, Paul Hand, Paul Pentland, Paul Wood, Richie Lamb, Ross MacIntosh, Scott Nicol, Scott Plews, Stanko Horansky, Steven Flockhart.

SHEFFIELD STEELERS

Andre Malo, Chris Kelland, Corey Beaulieu, Craig Chapman, Craig Lindsay, Dave Graham, David Longstaff, Derek Laxdal, Dion Del Monte, Ed Courtenay, Frank Kovacs, Glenn Mulvenna, Grant Sjerven, Hakan Falkenhall, Jamie Leach, Jamie Van der Horst, Jason Heywood, Jason Lafreniere, Jim Hibbert, John Wynne, Justin George, Kayle Short, Ken Priestlay, Les Millie, Mark Wright, Martin McKay, Mike O'Connor, Mike Ware, Neil Abel, Nicky Chinn, Perry Doyle, Piero Greco, Richard Uniacke, Rob Wilson, Ron Shudra, Scott Allison, Scott Campbell, Scott Heaton, Scott Neil, Steve Nemeth, Teeder Wynne, Tim Cranston, Tommy Plommer, Wayne Cowley.

AYR SCOTTISH EAGLES

Anders Hillstrom, Cam Bristow, Colin Ryder, David Trofimenkoff, Debb Carpenter, Derek Eberle, Dino Bauba, Ed Courtenay, Eric Murano, Geoff Sarjeant, Jamie Steer, Jan Mikel, Jim Mathieson, Johan Silfwerplatz, John Varga, Jonathan Weaver, Kevin Pozzo, Louis Dumont, Mark Montanari, Mike Bishop, Mike Harding, Patrick Lochi, Philippe DeRouville, Rhett Gordon, Rob Trumbley, Ryan Kummu, Scott Young, Shawn Byram, Shayne Stevenson, Stephen Foster, Teeder Wynne, Trevor Doyle, Vince Boe, Yuri Krivokhija, Yves Heroux.

DUNDEE STARS

Andrew Affleck, Andrew Finlay, Chris Conaboy, Craig Nelson, Dan Ratushny, Dominic Hopkins, Gary Dowd, Gary Wishart, Jan Mikel, Johan Boman, John Dolan, Ken Priestlay, Laurie Dunbar, Martin Wiita, Marty Hughes, Martyn Ford, Mike Harding, Mikko Inkinen, Nate Leslie, Patrick Lochi, Paul Berrington, Paul Sample, Scott Campbell, Scott Kirton, Scott Young, Slava Koulikov, Stephen Murphy, Stewart Rugg, Teeder Wynne, Tom Miller, Trevor Doyle.

EDINBURGH CAPITALS

Adrian Saul, Ali Flockhart, Ben Osborne, Blair Daly, Calum Baker, Calum McBride, Craig Wilson, Dale Howey, Daniel McIntyre, Dave Wakeling, David Beatson, Dino Bauba, Fredrick Oduya, Grant McPherson, Iain Beattie, Iain Robertson, Jan Krajicek, Jaroslav Prosvic, Jeff Marshall, Jim Vickers, Kevin Forshall, Ladislav Kudrna, Laurie Dunbar, Lee Coyle, Lewis Christie, Lewis Gasgon, Louis Christie, Martin Cingel, Martin Kucera, Matthew Rich, Michael Kiesman, Mike Clarke, Mike Sandbeck, Miroslav Droppa, Neil Hay, Neil McCann, Neil Stevenson-Moore, Paddy Lochi, Peter Konder, Ross Dalgliesh, Ross Hay, Ryan Ford, Scott Beeson, Stefan Nubert, Steven Francey, Steven Kaye, Steven Lynch, Travis Lisabeth.

BELFAST GIANTS

Chris McGimpsey, Curt Bowen, Curtis Huppe, Diarmuid Kelly, Fredrik Nasvall, George Awada, Graeme Walton, Bowen, Jason Ellery, Leigh Jamieson, Mel Angelstad, Marc Levers, Mark Morrison, Martin Klempa, Roman Gavalier, Shane Johnson, Todd Kelman.

MANCHESTER PHOENIX

Adam Radmall, Adam Walker, David Vychodil, Derek Campbell, James Hutchinson, Jason Wolfe, Joe Miller, Johan Molin, K.C. Timmons, Matt Compton, Radoslav Hecl, Robin Gomez, Ryan Watson, Scott Basiuk, Simon Mangos.

PLAYERS TONY HAS PLAYED
WITH FOR GREAT BRITAIN

Alistair Reid, Andre Malo, Andy Pickels, Anthony Johnson, Ashley Tait, Barry Hollhead, Brian Mason, Chris Kelland, Colin Shields, Craig Nelson, Dale Lambert, Damien Smith, Darren Hurley, David Clarke, David Graham, David Longstaff, Dean Edmiston, Doug McEwen, Gary Stefan, Gary Wishart, Glenn Mulvenna, Graham Waghorn, Grant Slater, Iain Robertson, Ian Cooper, Jamie Crapper, Jeff Hoad, Jeff Smith, Jimmy Hibbert, Joe Watkins, John 'Bernie' McCrone, John Iredale, John Lawless, Jonathan Weaver, Kevin Conway, Kevin MacNaught, Kyle Horne, Martin McKay, Merv Priest, Michael Tasker, Mike Bishop, Mike Ellis, Mike O'Connor, Moray Hanson, Neil Liddiard, Nicky Chinn, Patrick Scott, Paul Adey, Paul Berrington, Paul Dixon, Paul Hand, Paul Smith, Peter Smith, Phil Lee, Rick Brebant, Rick Fera, Rick Strachan, Rob Wilson, Scott Campbell, Scott Morrison, Scott Neil, Scott O'Connor, Scott Young, Shannon Hope, Shaun Johnson, Simon Hunt, Stephen Cooper, Stephen Johnson, Stephen Murphy, Steve Lyle, Steve Moria, Steve Thornton, Stevie Lyle, Terry Kurtenbach, Tim Cranston, Todd Bidner, Wayne Cowley.

PLAYERS DRAFTED TO EDMONTON OILERS WITH TONY IN 1986

Round Pick	Number	Name	Position	Club
1	#21	Kim Issel	Forward	Prince Albert Raiders (WHL)
2	#42	Jamie Nicolls	Forward	Portland Winter Hawks (WHL)
3	#63	Ron Shudra	Defence	Kamloops Blazers (WHL)
4	#84	Dan Currie	Forward	Sault-Ste.-Marie Greyhounds (OHL)
5	#105	David Haas	Forward	London Knights (OHL)
6	#126	Jim Ennis	Defence	Boston University (NCAA)
7	#147	Ivan Matulik	Forward	Bratislava Slovan Harvard (Slovak)
8	#168	Nick Beaulieu	Forward	Drummondville Voltigeurs (QMJHL)
9	#189	Mike Greenlay	Netminder	Calgary Midgets AAA
10	#210	Matt Lanza	Defence	Winthrop H.S. (Mass.)
11	#231	Mojmir Bozik	Defence	Kosice (Czech.)
12	#252	Tony Hand	Forward	Murrayfield Racers (BHL)

CLUB STATISTICS

TEAM	AUTUMN/CHALLENGE/KNOCKOUT CUPS				
Murrayfield Racers	GP	G	A	T	PIM
1981/82	-	-	-	-	-
1982/83	-	-	-	-	-
1983/84	7	12	8	20	4
1984/85	8	14	13	27	6
1985/86	9	22	23	45	15
1986/87	2	7	1	8	4
1987/88	6	16	12	28	6
1988/89	8	14	22	36	10
1989/90	7	11	16	27	12
1990/91	11	17	34	51	30
1991/92	2	1	7	8	0
1992/93	6	10	11	21	0
1993/94	11	12	24	36	20
Totals	77	136	171	307	107

TEAM		LEAGUE			
Murrayfield Racers	GP	G	A	T	PIM
1981/82	19	4	7	11	12
1982/83	22	18	21	39	23
1983/84	30	52	43	95	28
1984/85	36	72	92	164	36
1985/86	32	79	85	164	49
1986/87	35	105	111	216	86
1987/88	36	81	111	192	54
1988/89	35	86	126	212	57
1989/90	32	53	91	144	26
1990/91	34	60	96	156	46
1991/92	36	60	80	140	46
1992/93	35	66	119	185	100
1993/94	44	72	150	222	44
Totals	426	808	1,132	1,940	607

TEAM		CHAMPIONSHIP/PLAYOFF			
Murrayfield Racers	GP	G	A	T	PIM
1981/82	–	–	–	–	–
1982/83	2	2	1	3	0
1983/84	6	10	5	15	6
1984/85	6	13	11	24	4
1985/86	6	13	13	26	4
1986/87	6	9	19	28	4
1987/88	5	17	6	23	16
1988/89	4	8	10	18	12
1989/90	6	9	10	19	10
1990/91	7	8	17	25	8
1991/92	5	8	12	20	2
1992/93	7	14	19	33	8
1993/94	6	9	15	24	10
Totals	66	120	138	258	84

TEAM	AUTUMN/CHALLENGE/KNOCKOUT CUPS				
Edinburgh Racers	GP	G	A	T	PIM
1994/95	12	17	34	51	14
Totals	12	17	34	51	14

TEAM	LEAGUE				
Edinburgh Racers	GP	G	A	T	PIM
1994/95	42	71	136	207	28
Totals	42	71	136	207	28

TEAM	CHAMPIONSHIP/PLAYOFF				
Edinburgh Racers	GP	G	A	T	PIM
1994/95	8	13	21	34	20
Totals	8	13	21	34	20

TEAM	AUTUMN/CHALLENGE/KNOCKOUT CUPS				
Sheffield Steelers	GP	G	A	T	PIM
1995/96	12	23	18	41	12
1996/97	10	6	16	22	10
1997/98	12	6	14	20	2
1998/99	10	8	6	14	8
Totals	44	43	54	97	32

TEAM	LEAGUE				
Sheffield Steelers	GP	G	A	T	PIM
1995/96	35	46	77	123	65
1996/97	41	13	32	45	26
1997/98	28	9	30	39	16
1998/99	36	11	27	38	6
Totals	140	79	166	245	113

TEAM	CHAMPIONSHIP/PLAYOFF				
Sheffield Steelers	GP	G	A	T	PIM
1995/96	8	6	10	16	4
1996/97	8	3	6	9	4
1997/98	9	2	9	11	4
1998/99	5	1	4	5	0
Totals	30	12	29	41	12

TEAM	AUTUMN/CHALLENGE/KNOCKOUT CUPS				
Ayr Scottish Eagles	GP	G	A	T	PIM
1999/00	8	3	6	9	0
2000/01	8	3	5	8	14
Totals	16	6	11	17	14

TEAM	LEAGUE				
Ayr Scottish Eagles	GP	G	A	T	PIM
1999/00	40	8	35	43	52
2000/01	46	19	36	55	42
Totals	86	27	71	98	94

TEAM	CHAMPIONSHIP/PLAYOFF				
Ayr Scottish Eagles	GP	G	A	T	PIM
1999/00	7	0	4	4	0
2000/01	7	2	5	7	0
Totals	14	2	9	11	0

TEAM	AUTUMN/CHALLENGE/KNOCKOUT CUPS				
Dundee Stars	GP	G	A	T	PIM
2001/02	6	7	10	17	6
2002/03	10	7	15	22	6
Totals	16	14	25	39	12

TEAM		LEAGUE			
Dundee Stars	GP	G	A	T	PIM
2001/02	44	25	79	104	18
2002/03	36	22	58	80	99
Totals	80	47	137	184	117

TEAM		CHAMPIONSHIP/PLAYOFF			
Dundee Stars	GP	G	A	T	PIM
2001/02	10	7	17	24	4
2002/03	-	-	-	-	-
Totals	10	7	17	24	4

TEAM		AUTUMN/CHALLENGE/KNOCKOUT CUPS			
Edinburgh Capitals	GP	G	A	T	PIM
2003/04	12	5	13	18	16
2005/06	8	2	5	7	2
Totals	20	7	18	25	18

TEAM		LEAGUE			
Edinburgh Capitals	GP	G	A	T	PIM
2003/04	36	21	63	84	38
2005/06	43	14	37	51	2
Totals	79	35	100	135	40

TEAM		CHAMPIONSHIP/PLAYOFF			
Edinburgh Capitals	GP	G	A	T	PIM
2003/04	11	2	14	16	2
2005/06	4	2	2	4	0
Totals	15	4	16	20	2

TEAM	AUTUMN/CHALLENGE/KNOCKOUT CUPS				
Belfast Giants	GP	G	A	T	PIM
2004/05	-	-	-	-	-
Totals	-	-	-	-	-

TEAM	LEAGUE				
Belfast Giants	GP	G	A	T	PIM
2004/05	50	20	49	69	60
Totals	50	20	49	69	60

TEAM	CHAMPIONSHIP/PLAYOFF				
Belfast Giants	GP	G	A	T	PIM
2004/05	8	0	6	6	34
Totals	8	0	6	6	34

TEAM AUTUMN/CHALLENGE/KNOCKOUT CUPS					
SUMMARY	GP	G	A	T	PIM
Murrayfield Racers	77	136	171	307	107
Edinburgh Racers	12	17	34	51	14
Sheffield Steelers	44	43	54	97	32
Ayr Scottish Eagles	16	6	11	17	14
Dundee Stars	16	14	25	39	12
Edinburgh Capitals	20	7	18	25	18
Belfast Giants	-	-	-	-	-
Totals	185	223	313	536	197

TEAM SUMMARY	LEAGUE				
	GP	G	A	T	PIM
Murrayfield Racers	426	808	1,132	1,940	607
Edinburgh Racers	42	71	136	207	28
Sheffield Steelers	140	79	166	245	113
Ayr Scottish Eagles	86	27	71	98	94
Dundee Stars	80	47	137	184	117
Edinburgh Capitals	79	35	100	135	40
Belfast Giants	50	20	49	69	60
Totals	903	1,087	1,791	2,878	1,059

TEAM SUMMARY	CHAMPIONSHIP/PLAYOFF				
	GP	G	A	T	PIM
Murrayfield Racers	66	120	138	258	84
Sheffield Steelers	30	12	29	41	12
Ayr Scottish Eagles	14	2	9	11	0
Dundee Stars	10	7	17	24	4
Edinburgh Capitals	15	4	16	20	2
Belfast Giants	8	0	6	6	34
Totals	151	158	236	394	156

CLUB GRAND TOTAL:

GP	G	A	T	PIM
1,239	1,468	2,340	3,808	1,412

GB AND OTHER STATISTICS

GB INTERNATIONAL

World Championships	GP	G	A	T	PIM
1989	4	6	12	18	2
1990	4	5	8	13	0
1991	8	9	12	21	12
1992	5	6	12	18	4
1993	7	6	8	14	2
1994	6	0	0	0	0
1999	4	0	1	1	6
2000	7	2	8	10	2
2001	5	3	13	16	0
2002	5	2	4	6	2
Totals	55	40	78	118	30

Olympic Qualifier	GP	G	A	T	PIM
1993	4	0	2	2	4
Totals	4	0	2	2	4

GB JNR INTERNATIONAL

World Junior Championships	GP	G	A	T	PIM
1983/84	4	6	3	9	16
1985/86	5	10	1	11	6
1986/87	5	8	5	13	16
Totals	14	24	9	33	38

GB JNR EUROPEAN

European U19	GP	G	A	T	PIM
1981/82	4	6	4	10	14
Totals	4	6	4	10	14

European Junior Championships	GP	G	A	T	PIM
1983/84 (Silver)	6	9	7	16	4
Totals	6	9	7	16	4

SCOTLAND

Scotland *v.* England	GP	G	A	T	PIM
1983/84	1	1	2	3	n/a
1991/92	1	3	0	3	2
1992/93	1	2	1	3	n/a
1993/94	1	1	3	4	n/a
Totals	4	7	6	13	2

EUROPEAN CLUB

European Cup	GP	G	A	T	PIM
1984/85 (Dundee)	1	2	0	2	n/a
1987/88 (Murrayfield)	5	11	6	17	12
1988/89 (Murrayfield)	2	6	4	10	n/a
1995/96 (Sheffield)	3	3	3	6	n/a
1996/97 (Sheffield)	6	7	6	13	n/a
Totals	17	29	19	48	12

Continental Cup	GP	G	A	T	PIM
1998/99 (Sheffield)	3	1	0	1	n/a
Totals	3	1	0	1	n/a

OTHER

Victoria Cougars (WHL)	GP	G	A	T	PIM
1986/87	3	4	4	8	0
Totals	3	4	4	8	0

Other titles published by Stadia

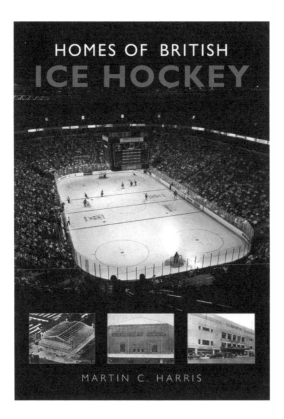

Homes of British Ice Hockey

MARTIN C. HARRIS

This book looks at every venue ever to host the sport in England, Scotland, Wales and Northern Ireland. Containing a wealth of information on each building, including team histories, statistical information, architectural details and many rare illustrations, this is a fascinating book for any follower of the sport.

0 7524 2581 1

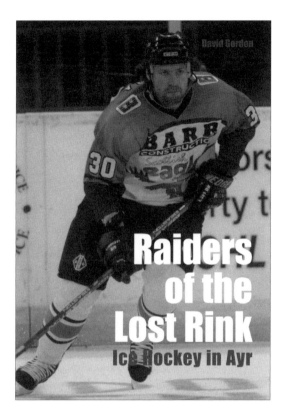

Raiders of the Lost Rink: Ice Hockey in Ayr
DAVID GORDON

The history of ice hockey in Ayr has been dramatic and turbulent since the town's first rink was opened in the 1930s. This absorbing and detailed account is rich in both anecdotes and statistics to chronicle the triumphs and tribulations of the sport in this Scottish west coast town over seventy-five years. Containing many rare photographs, it is an essential read for anyone with an interest in British ice hockey.

0 7524 3073 4

If you are interested in purchasing other books
published by Stadia, or in case you have difficulty finding
any Stadia books in your local bookshop, you can also place orders
directly through the Tempus Publishing website

www.tempus-publishing.com